I0007752

Chapter 1: Understanding the Power of Data Visualization and Storytelling

Data Visualization and storytelling have become integral components of business strategy, education, and communication. In an increasingly data-driven world, being able to effectively present and analyze data is essential for success. But what exactly is data visualization and storytelling, and why are they so powerful? In this chapter, we will delve into the purpose, benefits, and types of data visualization and storytelling, and explore how they can be used to create actionable insights.

Purpose

Data visualization is the graphical representation of data and information. It allows for complex data to be presented in a clear and understandable way, making it easier for viewers to process and interpret. On the other hand, storytelling is the art of using narrative to convey a message or information. It involves framing data within a context and providing a compelling narrative to bring it to life. Together, data visualization and storytelling create a powerful tool for communicating insights and driving action.

Benefits

There are numerous benefits to incorporating data visualization and storytelling into your presentations and analyses. First and foremost, they make complex data easy to understand and digest, cutting through the noise and presenting key insights in a visually appealing way. This leads to better understanding and retention of information, making it more likely for your message to be remembered and acted upon. Moreover, data visualization and storytelling can help to bridge the gap between data and human emotion. By presenting data in a narrative form, it becomes more relatable and can evoke an emotional response from the audience. This emotional connection can drive action and create a deeper understanding of the data being presented.In addition, data visualization and storytelling can bring together different perspectives and expertise. By using visuals to represent data, it becomes easier for individuals from different backgrounds to collaborate and contribute to the analysis. This can lead to more diverse and well-rounded insights.

Types

Data visualization and storytelling come in various forms and media. Some common types include charts, graphs, infographics, video presentations, and interactive dashboards. The type of visualization and storytelling used depends on the audience, message, and purpose. Charts and graphs are commonly used for presenting numerical data, such as sales figures or survey results. They can be simple or complex, depending on the amount of data being presented and the story you want to convey. Infographics, on the other hand, use a combination of visuals and text to present data in an engaging and informative way. They are often used in marketing or educational settings to present key statistics or concepts.Video presentations and animations can bring data to life by providing a visual narrative. They are particularly effective for demonstrating changes over time or complex patterns in data. Interactive dashboards allow viewers to explore the data on their own, making it more engaging and personalized.

In Conclusion

Data visualization and storytelling have become indispensable tools for creating actionable insights. They allow for complex data to be presented in an engaging and understandable way, making it easier for the audience to connect with the message and take action. In the following chapters, we will explore how to gather and prepare data, choose the right visualization tools, and incorporate storytelling techniques to maximize the impact of your data presentations. So let's dive in and discover the power of data visualization and storytelling together.

Chapter 2: Gathering and Preparing Data for

Analysis

Data is everywhere and it holds immense power. It is what drives businesses, shapes decisions, and creates impact. But with the sheer amount of data available, it can be overwhelming to know where to start. That's where data visualization and storytelling come in. In this chapter, we will explore the crucial steps of gathering and preparing data for analysis, to set the foundation for creating actionable insights.

Sources

The first step in any data analysis project is identifying the sources of your data. This can come from various places such as surveys, databases, social media platforms, or even physical records. The key is to determine which sources are relevant and useful for your analysis. It's important to carefully select your sources as they will have a direct impact on the insights you are able to draw from your data.When selecting sources, it's also important to consider the quality and accuracy of the data. Data can often be biased or incomplete, leading to flawed insights. It's crucial to thoroughly vet your sources to ensure the integrity of your data.

Cleaning

Once you have identified your sources, the next step is to clean the data. This is a critical step as it helps to eliminate any errors or inconsistencies in your data, ensuring that it is accurate and reliable.Data cleaning involves various processes such as removing duplicate entries, correcting spelling errors, and filling in missing data. It can be a time-consuming task, but it ultimately leads to more accurate insights and saves time in the long run.

Formatting

Data comes in various formats and it's essential to format it in a way that is suitable for analysis. This involves organizing the data into a structured and standardized format, making it easier to work with. Formatting also includes converting data into visual formats such as tables, charts, or graphs. This is where the power of data visualization comes into play, as it allows for a more intuitive and effective way of presenting data.When formatting data, it's important to consider the end goal of your analysis. Will it be presented to a specific audience or used for a particular purpose? This will help determine the most appropriate format for your data.

Conclusion

Gathering and preparing data may seem like a tedious and technical process, but it is crucial to the success of your data analysis. By carefully selecting sources, cleaning and formatting your data, you are setting the foundation for creating impactful and actionable insights. Remember, the quality of your data directly impacts the quality of your insights, so it's important to invest time and effort into this crucial step. In the next chapter, we will delve into the various tools available for data visualization and how to choose the right ones for your project.

Chapter 3: Choosing the Right Visualization Tools

Choosing the right visualization tools is crucial for effectively presenting data and telling a compelling story. In this chapter, we will dive into the three most commonly used tools for data visualization: infographics, charts, and maps. We will explore the benefits and drawbacks of each tool, and provide tips and best practices for creating visually appealing and impactful visualizations.

Infographics

Infographics have become increasingly popular in recent years, and for good reason. These visual representations of information combine text, data, and graphics to create an easy-to-understand and visually appealing format. Infographics can take complex data and distill it into bite-sized pieces, making it more accessible for a wider audience. One of the key benefits of infographics is their ability to tell a story in a concise and engaging manner. The graphics and visuals used in infographics help to draw the reader's attention and keep them engaged, while the data and text provide essential information and context. This combination creates a powerful tool for storytelling. However, infographics can also have drawbacks if not executed properly. One common mistake is overcrowding the design with too much information. This can overwhelm the reader and make the infographic difficult to follow. It's important to carefully select the data and visuals that best support the story you want to tell.When creating infographics, it's important to consider the design elements, such as color, typography, and layout. These elements play a key role in catching the reader's eye and creating a cohesive and visually appealing design. Using a consistent color scheme and font throughout the infographic can also enhance its readability and make it more visually appealing.

Charts

Charts are another popular tool for data visualization and are great for presenting numerical data in a visual format. They come in various forms, such as bar graphs, pie charts, line graphs, and scatter plots. Each type of chart serves a specific purpose, and it's important to understand when and how to use them effectively. The key benefit of using charts is their ability to quickly and effectively display numerical data. They make it easy for the reader to compare and understand data points, trends, and patterns. Charts are also highly flexible, allowing for customization and visual enhancements to better tell the story behind the data. However, charts can be misleading if not used correctly. One common mistake is not properly labeling axes, which can distort the data and lead to inaccurate conclusions. It's also important to choose the right type of chart for the data being presented. For example, a pie chart is not suitable for comparing more than a few data points, while a bar graph may be more effective for showing changes over time.When designing charts, it's important to choose colors that are easy on the eyes and make it easy to differentiate between different data sets. Labels and annotations should also be used to provide context and guide the reader's understanding.

Maps

Maps have been used for centuries to visually represent geographical data and show the relationships between different locations. In today's digital age, maps have become even more versatile and can be used in various forms, such as interactive maps, heat maps, and 3D maps. The key advantage of using maps for data visualization is their ability to show spatial relationships and patterns that may not be evident in other types of visualizations. Maps can also be highly interactive, allowing readers to zoom in and out and explore data in more detail. However, maps can be challenging to create and may require a higher level of technical expertise compared to other tools. They also have limitations, such as only being able to represent numerical data for a specific geographical area. It's important to carefully consider whether a map is the right visualization tool for the data being presented.When creating maps, it's important to choose the right type of map for the data being presented. For example, a heat map may be more effective for showing concentration and density of data points, while a choropleth map can be used to show data for specific regions. The color scheme and key for the map should also be carefully selected to ensure the data is accurately represented.

Conclusion

When choosing the right visualization tool, it's important to consider the data being presented, the audience, and the story you want to tell. Infographics, charts, and maps each have their own strengths and limitations, and understanding how to use them effectively can greatly enhance the impact of your data presentation. By carefully selecting the most appropriate tool and incorporating design principles, you can create visually appealing and engaging visualizations that effectively communicate your message.

Chapter 4: The Art of Tailoring Your Message for Effective Data Visualization and Storytelling

Data without context is meaningless. It's like a canvas without paint, a stage without actors, or a symphony without instruments. In order for data to have impact, it needs to be presented in a way that speaks to your audience. This is where the art of data visualization and storytelling comes into play. In this chapter, we will dive into the key aspects of targeting your audience, communicating effectively, and making your data relevant in order to create actionable insights through data visualization and storytelling.

Target demographics

Before we can even begin to think about how to communicate our data, we first need to understand who we are communicating to. Knowing your target demographic is crucial when it comes to data visualization and storytelling. This includes understanding their age, gender, education level, interests, and any other relevant characteristics that may influence how they interpret and engage with data. For example, a presentation on financial data to a group of millennials may require a different approach compared to presenting the same data to a group of older individuals from the Baby Boomer generation. Millennials may be more interested in interactive visualizations and infographics, while older individuals may prefer more traditional charts and graphs. By understanding your target demographic, you can tailor your data visualization and storytelling techniques to appeal to their specific needs and preferences.But it's not just about understanding demographics, it's also about understanding your audience's mindset. Are they data-savvy or more visual learners? Are they analytical or more emotionally-driven? Knowing these things can help you choose the most effective data visualization and storytelling methods to engage and resonate with your audience.

Communication styles

Now that we have a better understanding of our target demographic, we can begin to think about how to effectively communicate our data to them. Communication is a two-way street, and as the presenter, it's important to find a balance between being informative and engaging. One of the most powerful ways to communicate data is through storytelling. It allows us to humanize the data and make it relatable to our audience. Whether it's through a personal anecdote, a powerful narrative, or a compelling metaphor, storytelling can help make even the most complex data more understandable and memorable.In addition to storytelling, incorporating multiple communication styles can also be beneficial. This can include using visuals, such as charts, graphs, and infographics, along with verbal explanations and interactive elements. By using a combination of these techniques, you can cater to different learning styles and keep your audience engaged throughout the data presentation.

Relevance

Last but certainly not least, making your data relevant to your audience is key to creating actionable insights. Your data may be incredibly insightful and well-presented, but if it doesn't speak to your audience's needs and interests, it will not have the desired impact. To make your data relevant, it's important to tie it back to your audience's goals, challenges, and interests. Ask yourself, "Why should they care about this data?" and "What actions can they take based on this data?" By answering these questions, you can ensure that your data is not only informative but also actionable. In order to make your data relevant, it's also important to consider the current societal and cultural context. What's happening in the world right now that may influence how your audience perceives and responds to your data? By staying up-to-date on current events and trends, you can better tailor your data visualization and storytelling to be timely and relevant to your audience.

In conclusion, targeting your audience, communicating effectively, and making your data relevant are essential elements to creating impactful data visualization and storytelling. By understanding your audience's demographics, using various communication styles, and making your data relevant, you can create actionable insights that inspire change and drive action. Remember, data isn't just about numbers and charts, it's about telling a story that resonates with your audience and drives them to action.

Chapter 5: The Art of Data Visualization and Storytelling

Narrative Structure: Crafting a Compelling Story with Data

Data is more than just numbers and statistics, it has the power to tell a powerful story. As a data storyteller, it is your job to weave together all the data points and create a narrative that captivates your audience. But how do you create a compelling story with data?Firstly, it is important to have a clear and defined structure for your data story. This will help guide the audience and make the information more digestible. Start with a hook to grab their attention – a startling statistic or an intriguing question. Then, introduce your characters - the data points or variables - and their relationships. This will help establish a framework for your story. From there, build up the tension and conflict of your data story. What are the challenges being faced? What is at stake? This will keep your audience engaged and invested in the outcome. Use visual aids such as charts, graphs, and images to enhance your story and make the data more relatable. As you reach the climax of your data story, reveal the most important insights and revelations. This is where your storytelling skills really come into play. Use powerful language and emotional appeals to convey the significance of these insights. Paint a vivid picture for your audience and make them feel the impact of the data.Finally, wrap up your data story with a meaningful conclusion. Tie back to your hook and leave your audience with a call to action. Whether it is a change in behavior, a shift in perspective, or a call for action, a strong conclusion will ensure that your data story stays with your audience long after they have left the presentation.

Emotional Appeals: Connecting with Your Audience on a Deeper Level

Data may be cold and factual, but storytelling has the power to evoke strong emotions in your audience. Emotions are a key factor in decision making and can greatly influence the way your audience perceives the data. As such, it is important for data storytellers to tap into the emotional elements of their data to connect with their audience on a deeper level. One way to do this is through the use of personal anecdotes and real-life examples that demonstrate the impact of the data. These human stories provide a relatable and emotional connection to the data, making it more memorable and impactful. Use language that is rich in emotion and sensory details to evoke specific feelings in your audience. Consider using metaphors and analogies to simplify complex data and make it more relatable. Another effective way to appeal to emotions is through the use of visual aids. As the old saying goes, a picture is worth a thousand words. A well-designed and visually appealing data visualization can evoke strong emotions and create a more immersive experience for your audience. Use colors, shapes, and images to communicate the emotional tone of your data story.Remember, emotions are not just limited to positive ones. Sometimes, using negative emotions such as fear, anger, or sadness can also be effective in driving action and change. Be aware of the tone and message you want to convey and tailor your emotional appeals accordingly.

Persuasive Elements: Convincing Your Audience to Take Action

The ultimate goal of data visualization and storytelling is to influence the audience and drive action. As a data storyteller, you need to be persuasive in your delivery to convince your audience to take action based on the insights presented. One way to do this is by using a storytelling technique called the "Rule of Three". This involves presenting three key takeaways or recommendations based on your data, to make it more memorable and compelling. People tend to remember things in threes and it also adds a sense of authority and confidence to your presentation. In addition, use data to back up your claims and recommendations. This adds credibility to your story and makes it more convincing. Visual representations of data, such as charts, can make the information more digestible and easier to grasp. Use these visuals to support your argument and provide evidence for your recommendations. Lastly, consider the language and tone of your data story. Using positive and empowering language can motivate your audience to take action and make a difference. Make your audience feel like they are part of the solution and emphasize the impact of their actions. This will make them more likely to act on the insights presented in your data story.

In conclusion, mastering the art of data visualization and storytelling involves crafting a compelling narrative, appealing to emotions, and being persuasive in your delivery. By incorporating these elements into your data stories, you can create a powerful and impactful experience for your audience. So go forth and use the power of data storytelling to create meaningful and actionable insights.

Chapter 6: Creating Actionable Insights through Data Visualization and Storytelling

Bringing Numbers to Life

Data is a powerful tool that can provide valuable insights and inform decision-making in any industry. But often, raw data can be overwhelming and difficult to understand, especially for non-technical individuals. This is where data visualization comes in – creating compelling and visually appealing representations of data that bring numbers to life and make them easily digestible.Visuals have the ability to communicate complex information in a way that is easy to understand and retain. They can turn dry statistics into vibrant, engaging stories that captivate the audience and truly bring the numbers to life. Whether it is through charts, graphs, or interactive dashboards, data visualization adds a visual layer to data that helps to simplify and clarify the message.

Creating Context

Numbers alone do not tell the full story – they need to be put into context in order to derive meaningful insights. Data visualization can help with that by providing a visual representation of relationships between different data points. For example, a simple line graph can show the correlation between two variables, while a scatter plot can demonstrate patterns and trends in the data.By adding context to data, data visualization can aid in understanding the bigger picture and uncover hidden insights that may have otherwise gone unnoticed. This deeper understanding can lead to better decision-making and ultimately, more impactful outcomes.

Adding Depth and Meaning

One of the main goals of data visualization and storytelling is to make data more meaningful and impactful. As humans, we are wired to respond to stories – they engage our minds and emotions, making us more receptive to the information being presented. By incorporating storytelling techniques into data visualization, we can create a more powerful and memorable message. Data storytelling involves using a narrative structure to present data in a way that guides the audience to a specific conclusion or action. This can be achieved through various techniques such as adding annotations, using metaphors or analogies, or incorporating real-life examples. These elements can add depth and meaning to the data, making it more relatable and impactful for the audience. In addition, data visualization can also help to break down complex concepts and present them in a more simplified manner. This allows for a deeper understanding and makes it easier for individuals to connect with the data and its implications.In today's digital age, data is being generated at an unprecedented rate. However, without proper visualization and storytelling, data can remain hidden and its true potential untapped. By bringing numbers to life, providing context, and adding depth and meaning, data visualization and storytelling can transform raw data into actionable insights that drive positive change.

Chapter 7: Design Principles for Effective Visualizations

Visualizing data is both an art and a science. It requires a delicate balance between creativity and technical skill. As technology continues to advance, the possibilities for visualizing data are endless. However, with so many options available, it can be overwhelming to know where to start. That's where design principles for effective visualizations come into play. By following some fundamental guidelines, you can create stunning and impactful visualizations that effectively communicate your message.

Color

Color plays a vital role in any visualization. It not only adds visual appeal but also helps to convey meaning and highlight important information. When choosing colors for your visualization, it's essential to consider the emotions and feelings associated with different shades. Bright and bold colors can evoke excitement and energy, while muted or pastel tones can create a sense of calm and sophistication. It's also crucial to use a color palette that is visually appealing and helps to differentiate data points. Experimenting with different color combinations can help you find the perfect balance for your visualization.

Layout

The layout of your visualization is critical for ensuring that it is easy to understand and visually appealing. A cluttered layout can make it challenging to comprehend the information being presented, whereas a well-organized layout can make it easier for the viewer to digest the data. When designing your layout, it's essential to consider the principles of visual hierarchy. This means using size, color, and placement to draw attention to the most critical elements of your visualization. The use of negative space can also help to enhance the overall look and feel of your visualization.

Fonts

The right font can make all the difference in the readability and impact of your visualization. It's essential to choose a font that is easy to read and complements the style of your visualization. Avoid using too many different fonts as it can make your visualization look messy and uncoordinated. Stick to two or three fonts at most and use them consistently throughout your visualization. Sans-serif fonts, such as Arial or Helvetica, are popular choices for data visualizations due to their simplicity and readability.

Visual Consistency

Consistency is crucial when it comes to designing effective visualizations. This means using the same style, colors, fonts, and layout throughout your visualization to maintain a cohesive look. If you're working with a team, it's essential to establish style guidelines to ensure that everyone is on the same page. Visual consistency not only makes your visualization more visually appealing but also helps to avoid confusion and ensures that the focus remains on the data.

Less is More

One common mistake when visualizing data is trying to include too much information at once. While it may seem beneficial to include as much information as possible, it can actually have the opposite effect by overwhelming the viewer. Instead, focus on the most critical data points and keep your visualization simple. This will make it easier for your audience to interpret the data and understand the story you're trying to tell.

Use Visual Metaphors

Sometimes, data can be dry and difficult to understand. That's where using visual metaphors can come in handy. A visual metaphor is using an object or image to represent something more abstract or complex. For example, using a tree to represent a company's growth over time. Visual metaphors can add depth and meaning to your visualization and make it more engaging for your audience.

Make it Interactive

Interactive visualizations are becoming increasingly popular as they allow the viewer to engage with the data and gain more insights. Adding interactive elements such as hover effects, clickable buttons, or scrollable timelines can make your visualization more dynamic and interesting. However, it's essential to use interactive features purposefully and not to overload your visualization with unnecessary animations.

Accessibility

When designing visualizations, it's crucial to keep accessibility in mind. This means ensuring that your visualization can be easily understood by all audiences, including those with visual impairments. Some tips for making your visualization more accessible include using alt text for images, providing a high-contrast option for colorblind viewers, and using large and legible fonts.

Testing and Feedback

Designing effective visualizations is an ongoing process. It's essential to test your visualization with a sample audience and gather feedback to further improve it. Consider usability tests, where you observe how users interact and understand your visualization, or gather feedback from your target audience through surveys. This will help you identify any areas for improvement and fine-tune your visualization before its final release.

In conclusion, effective visualizations require a balance of creativity, technical skill, and adherence to design principles. By considering factors such as color, layout, fonts, and visual consistency, you can create visually appealing and impactful visualizations that effectively communicate your message to your audience. Remember to keep it simple, use visual metaphors, and always seek feedback to continuously improve your visualizations. With these principles in mind, you can take your data visualizations to the next level and make a lasting impression on your audience.

Chapter 8: Creating Beautiful Visualizations with Hierarchical Data, Time Series, and Correlations

Hierarchical data, time series, and correlations are powerful tools for organizing and analyzing complex data sets. When incorporated into data visualization, they can provide rich insights and tell compelling stories. In this chapter, we will explore how to effectively use these techniques to create beautiful and impactful visualizations.

Hierarchical Data

In today's world, data is everywhere. We are constantly bombarded with information from a variety of sources, making it increasingly difficult to find patterns and make sense of it all. Hierarchical data provides a way to structure and organize complex data, making it easier to comprehend and analyze. One way to represent hierarchical data is through tree maps, where each node represents a specific category and its subcategories are shown as nested rectangles. This type of visualization allows us to see the relationships between categories and compare them visually. Another popular approach for hierarchical data is sunburst charts, where the innermost ring represents the top-level category and each ring outward represents its subcategories. This type of visualization is useful for showing the distribution of data within each category and how they contribute to the overall picture.When designing visualizations with hierarchical data, it's important to think about the hierarchy of information and the most effective way to present it. It's also crucial to ensure that the visualizations are easy to navigate and understand, so the audience can quickly grasp the key insights.

Time Series

Time series refers to data that is collected over a period of time, usually at regular intervals. It can come in many forms, such as stock prices, weather data, or website traffic. Analyzing time series data can provide valuable insights into trends, patterns, and relationships between variables. One common way to visualize time series data is through line charts. They allow for easy comparison of multiple data sets over time and can also show changes and trends in data. Another effective approach is to use stacked area charts, which allow us to see how different categories contribute to changes over time.A more advanced technique for visualizing time series data is through animation. By animating data, we can see how variables change and how they relate to each other in a dynamic way. This can be especially useful for complex data sets with multiple variables.

Correlations

Correlation is the relationship between two variables, and can range from positive to negative. Visualizing correlations can help us understand the strength of the relationship and identify any patterns or trends. One way to visualize correlations is through scatter plots, which use dots to represent individual data points and show the relationship between two variables. Another approach is to use heat maps, where the size and color of the squares represent the strength of the correlation.It's important to note that correlation does not necessarily imply causation. Therefore, it's crucial to carefully interpret correlations and avoid making assumptions based on them. Including clear labels and context in the visualization can also help prevent misinterpretation.

In Conclusion

In this chapter, we have explored the power of hierarchical data, time series, and correlations in data visualization. By understanding how to effectively use these techniques, we can create beautiful and informative visualizations that tell compelling stories. Remember to keep the audience in mind and carefully consider the best way to present the data to ensure maximum impact. With these tools in our toolkit, we can unlock the full potential of data visualization.

Chapter 9: Data Visualization for User Engagement, Navigation, and Dynamic Updates

In today's digital age, data is constantly flowing and being created at an unprecedented rate. With this influx of information, it is vital for businesses and organizations to effectively present and communicate their data to their audiences. This is where data visualization comes in - using visual tools to make complex data more digestible and engaging for viewers. In this chapter, we will dive into how data visualization can enhance user engagement, aid navigation, and provide dynamic updates for your data presentation.

User Engagement

Data visualization is more than just making numbers look pretty - it is a powerful tool for increasing user engagement. When presented with a text-heavy report or spreadsheet, the viewer's attention and interest can quickly diminish. However, a well-designed data visualization can capture and maintain their attention, making them more likely to absorb and retain the information. Furthermore, visuals have a higher chance of being shared and remembered, especially in today's social media-driven world.When creating data visualizations for user engagement, it is important to keep your audience in mind. Not all visuals resonate with everyone, so it is crucial to understand your target demographic and what type of visual they respond to best. For example, younger audiences may prefer more interactive and dynamic visualizations, while older audiences may prefer more traditional charts and graphs. By tailoring your visuals to your audience, you can ensure maximum engagement and impact.

Navigation

In addition to engaging users, data visualization can also aid in navigation and understanding of complex data. With the abundance of data available, it can be overwhelming for viewers to sift through and make sense of it all. However, by using visualizations, you can guide viewers through the data in a more organized and structured manner.Charts and graphs can help categorize data and identify patterns and trends, making it easier for viewers to grasp the overall message. Visualizations can also provide a hierarchy of information, allowing viewers to delve deeper into specific data points if desired. With the use of interactive visualizations, viewers can also have control over what data they want to see, further enhancing their navigation experience.

Dynamic Updates

One of the greatest benefits of data visualization is its ability to provide dynamic updates. With traditional reports or spreadsheets, updating data and making changes can be time-consuming and tedious. However, with visualizations, the data can be connected to a live data source, allowing for real-time updates. This is especially useful in scenarios where data is constantly changing, such as in financial markets or social media analytics.By providing dynamic updates, visualizations can keep users informed and up-to-date with the latest information. This can be valuable for decision-making and identifying patterns and trends in the data. Furthermore, dynamic visualizations can also provide a level of transparency and credibility, as viewers can see the data in its raw form and have confidence in its accuracy.

From engaging users to aiding navigation and providing dynamic updates, data visualization is a powerful tool in effectively presenting data. By understanding your audience, using visuals to guide navigation, and providing live updates, you can ensure that your data is not only understood but also retained and acted upon. In the next chapter, we will explore ethical considerations when using data visualization.

Chapter 10: Incorporating Data Visualization into Business Strategy

Data is at the heart of every business. From customer information to sales data, organizations are constantly collecting and analyzing data to make informed decisions and drive growth. However, even with the abundance of data, it can be challenging for businesses to make sense of it all and use it to their advantage. This is where data visualization comes in – a powerful tool that enables businesses to turn complex data into actionable insights.Data visualization is not just about creating beautiful charts and graphs. It goes beyond that, incorporating accuracy, transparency, and bias to effectively communicate insights in a way that resonates with decision-makers. In fact, a study by MIT Sloan Management Review found that companies that consistently use data visualization are more likely to have higher financial performance.

Accuracy

Accuracy is essential when it comes to data visualization. Inaccurate or misleading visualizations can lead to incorrect conclusions and ultimately, poor decision-making. Therefore, it is crucial for businesses to ensure that the data used for visualization is accurate and relevant to the intended purpose. One way to ensure accuracy is by regularly auditing the data used for visualization. This involves verifying the source of the data, checking for inconsistencies and errors, and validating its relevance to the business goal. Additionally, businesses should also be transparent about their data sources and how it has been collected, processed, and analyzed.Furthermore, businesses should also pay attention to outlier data points that could skew the overall visualization. Outliers can significantly impact the accuracy of a visualization and should be carefully considered and addressed to avoid misleading conclusions.

Transparency

Transparency goes hand in hand with accuracy in data visualization. It is crucial for businesses to be transparent about the processes involved in creating a visualization to build trust and credibility with decision-makers. A transparent approach involves explaining how the visualization has been created, including the tools and techniques used. This allows decision-makers to understand the limitations and potential biases of the data and visualization techniques used. It also allows for open discussions and corrections if needed.Businesses should also be transparent about the limitations of the data used for visualization. For instance, if there is missing data or a small sample size, this should be clearly stated to avoid misinterpretation of the visualization.

Bias

One of the most significant challenges in data visualization is dealing with bias. Bias is inherent in data, and it can influence the visualization and the conclusions drawn from it. Bias can come from various sources, such as human error, subjective data collection, or even the visualization techniques used. To address bias in data visualization, businesses should strive for diverse data collection and analysis. This involves considering different perspectives and sources of data to create a well-rounded visualization that is less likely to be influenced by bias.Additionally, businesses should also be aware of their own biases and seek to minimize their impact on the visualization process. This can be done by involving a diverse team in the creation of visualizations and regularly reassessing the visualization techniques used to ensure they are not unintentionally amplifying bias.

Incorporating Data Visualization into Business Strategy

Data visualization has value beyond just presenting insights to decision-makers. It can also be incorporated into a business's overall strategy to drive growth and success. By using visualizations, businesses can identify trends, patterns, and relationships in their data, which can inform strategic decisions. For instance, businesses can use data visualization to gain a better understanding of their target audience's preferences and behaviors, helping them create more targeted and effective marketing strategies. It can also assist with identifying areas of improvement in business processes and identifying potential risks to make proactive decisions.Furthermore, businesses can also use data visualization to communicate their performance and progress to stakeholders. Instead of relying on lengthy reports and spreadsheets, visualizations can provide a clear and engaging snapshot of a business's performance, highlighting successes and areas for improvement.

The Future of Data Visualization in Business

As technology continues to advance, so does the field of data visualization. In the future, we can expect to see more incorporation of artificial intelligence and machine learning in data visualization, making it even easier for businesses to extract insights from vast amounts of data. Immersive technologies, such as virtual and augmented reality, also have the potential to revolutionize data visualization in business. These technologies can provide a more interactive and engaging experience, allowing decision-makers to explore data in a more intuitive way.

In conclusion, data visualization is a crucial tool for businesses looking to turn complex data into actionable insights. By incorporating accuracy, transparency, and addressing bias, businesses can create effective visualizations that drive success and inform strategic decisions. As technology continues to evolve, data visualization will only become more critical in helping businesses make sense of their data and stay ahead of the competition.

Chapter 11: Presenting Data to Non-Technical Audiences

Simplifying Jargon

Data visualization can be a daunting and overwhelming subject for those who are not familiar with the technical jargon. As storytellers, it is our responsibility to simplify complex terms and techniques in order to effectively communicate with non-technical audiences. One way to do this is by using familiar and relatable examples to explain data visualization concepts. For instance, instead of using technical terms such as "scatter plot" or "pie chart", we can explain them as a visual representation of a group of data points or a graph divided into slices that represent different categories. This not only makes the information more digestible, but it also helps to engage our audience by tying in real-life examples that they can relate to.It is also important to avoid using acronyms and abbreviations that may be common in our industry, but unfamiliar to non-technical audiences. If it is necessary to use them, make sure to provide a clear definition and explanation.

Providing Context

Data without context is like a puzzle with missing pieces. It may look interesting, but it is difficult to understand the bigger picture. This is why it is crucial to provide context when presenting data to non-technical audiences. Context helps to add meaning and relevance to the data being presented. It answers the question of "why" the data is important and how it relates to the audience. For example, instead of just displaying sales numbers for a particular product, we can provide context by including information about the market trends, competition, and consumer behavior. This allows the audience to see the bigger picture and understand the impact of the data being presented.Another way to provide context is by using storytelling techniques. By incorporating a narrative, we can create an emotional connection with the data and make it more relatable to the audience. This not only helps engage the audience, but it also aids in better retention and understanding of the data.

Communicating Uncertainty

One of the challenges of presenting data to non-technical audiences is the fear of overwhelming them with complex and uncertain information. As data storytellers, it is our responsibility to communicate uncertainty in a transparent and honest manner. One way to do this is by using visual aids such as error bars or confidence intervals to represent the margin of error in the data. This allows the audience to see the range of possible outcomes and understand the level of uncertainty in the data being presented.Another important aspect is to explain the limitations and assumptions of the data. This helps to set realistic expectations and prevents any misleading interpretations. It is also important to be transparent about any biases in the data and provide alternate perspectives to ensure a well-rounded understanding.

Conclusion

In conclusion, presenting data to non-technical audiences requires a combination of simplifying jargon, providing context, and communicating uncertainty. It is our responsibility, as data storytellers, to make information easily understandable and relatable for our audience. By incorporating these techniques, we can break down complex data into meaningful and actionable insights that can drive change and create impact.

Chapter 12: Storytelling with Data for Action and Change

Data visualization is a powerful tool for conveying information and telling stories. When used effectively, it has the ability to inspire action and drive change. In this chapter, we will explore how data visualization can be harnessed for creating actionable insights, and the importance of incorporating storytelling techniques into the process.

Call to Action

As a data storyteller, your ultimate goal is to inspire action and drive change. But how do you do this effectively? The key lies in crafting a compelling call to action that motivates your audience to take the desired action. One way to achieve this is by creating a sense of urgency. By highlighting the importance and timeliness of the issue at hand, you can invoke a sense of responsibility and compel people to take action. Your call to action should also be specific and clearly outline the steps that need to be taken.For example, if your data visualization reveals a concerning trend in environmental pollution, your call to action could be to reduce plastic waste by using reusable bags and bottles. By providing a specific action, you make it easier for people to participate and contribute to the cause.

Creating Urgency

Creating urgency is a crucial aspect of storytelling with data. Without a sense of urgency, your message may fall flat and fail to motivate action. To create urgency, you must first connect with your audience. This means understanding their values, needs, and concerns. Once you have established this connection, you can then use data to illustrate the urgency of the issue. For example, if you are working with a non-profit organization that focuses on saving endangered animals, you can use data to show the decline in the population of a particular species. This data can be accompanied by a call to action, such as donating to the cause or taking part in conservation efforts.By creating a sense of urgency through data, you can increase the impact of your storytelling and inspire people to take meaningful action.

Engaging with Stakeholders

Effective data storytelling not only involves engaging with your target audience but also with stakeholders who have a vested interest in your message. These stakeholders may include decision-makers, partners, or community members. Engaging with stakeholders requires a strategic approach that takes into account their needs and concerns. This may involve presenting data in a way that is relevant and meaningful to them, using storytelling techniques to make the message more relatable, and involving them in the process of creating actionable insights. By engaging with stakeholders, you not only ensure that your message is well-received, but you also increase the chances of it being acted upon. When stakeholders are invested in your cause, they are more likely to take action and drive change.

In conclusion, data visualization and storytelling, when used together, have the power to inspire action and drive change. By crafting a compelling call to action, creating a sense of urgency, and engaging with stakeholders, you can make your data visualization truly impactful and contribute towards making a positive difference in the world. So go forth and tell your data stories with passion and purpose, for they have the potential to change the world.

Chapter 13: Infographics for Non-Visual Data

Infographics are a powerful tool for communicating complex information in a visually appealing and easily digestible format. They combine data, images, and text to tell a story and present information in a way that is both engaging and informative. However, most infographics are designed to display visual data, such as charts, graphs, and maps. But what about non-visual data? How can we use infographics to tell a story with data that cannot be represented visually?

Using Text

Text is a fundamental element of any infographic, but it can also be used to convey data and tell a story on its own. Text can be used to summarize data, provide context, and guide the reader through the information presented. When working with non-visual data, it is essential to craft a compelling and concise narrative with your text. Use descriptive language, and consider the tone and style of writing to convey the emotions and impact of the data.It is also essential to format the text in a visually appealing way that is easy to read. Use headings, subheadings, and bullet points to break up the text and create a flow that guides the reader through the information. Don't be afraid to get creative with fonts, sizes, and colors to make the text visually engaging and aligned with your overall infographic design.

Using Icons

Icons are a powerful way to represent data and ideas in a simple and straightforward manner. When working with non-visual data, icons can be a useful tool for conveying information that may be difficult to visualize. For example, if your data is on the emotional well-being of college students, using icons to represent different moods and feelings can enhance the reader's understanding and emotional connection to the data.Icons can also be used to break up text and add visual interest to an infographic. Consider using icons as dividers between sections or as a way to represent data points in a visually appealing way. Just make sure to choose icons that are relevant and easy to understand for your target audience.

Using Charts

While charts and graphs are typically used to display visual data, they can also be helpful when working with non-visual data. Bar charts, for example, can be used to compare different data points in a visually engaging way. Line graphs can also be utilized to show trends over time, even if the data being represented is non-visual.Additionally, charts and graphs can also be used to present the results of surveys or polls. You can use pie charts to display percentages or bar graphs to compare different responses. The key is to keep the design simple and easy to understand, so the focus remains on the data itself.

Bringing it All Together

When using infographics to communicate non-visual data, it is crucial to strike a balance between text, icons, and charts. Each element should work together to create a cohesive and impactful story, rather than competing for the reader's attention. Utilize design principles such as color, hierarchy, and balance to create a visually appealing infographic that effectively conveys the information presented.It is also essential to consider the target audience when designing an infographic for non-visual data. The tone, language, and design should align with the audience's interests and needs to ensure the message is received and understood.

Incorporating Interactivity

With advancements in technology, infographics can now be designed to incorporate interactive elements. This can be especially useful when working with non-visual data, as it allows the reader to engage with the information in a more immersive way. Interactive elements can include animations, clickable data points, or quizzes to test the reader's understanding of the data.Not only does interactivity make the infographic more engaging, but it also allows for a deeper level of understanding and connection to the data. As the saying goes, "A picture is worth a thousand words," and interactive infographics take this to a whole new level by allowing the reader to experience and interact with the data in a meaningful way.

Final Thoughts

Infographics are a versatile and powerful tool for communicating data visually. While they are often used to display visual data, they can also be effective in telling a story with non-visual data. With the right combination of text, icons, charts, and interactive elements, infographics can bring to life even the most complex and abstract data. So next time you are faced with presenting non-visual data, consider using infographics to create an engaging and impactful story.

Chapter 14: Visualizing Big Data

The rise of digital technology and the widespread use of internet-connected devices have led to a massive increase in the amount of data being generated and collected. This has resulted in the term "big data" becoming a buzzword in today's society. Big data refers to the large and complex sets of data that traditional data processing and analysis methods are unable to handle. As businesses and organizations are faced with this explosion of data, the need for effective visualization techniques to make sense of it all has become more crucial than ever. In this chapter, we will explore the challenges, techniques, and solutions for visualizing big data.

Challenges

The challenge of visualizing big data lies in its sheer volume and complexity. It can be overwhelming to make sense of thousands or even millions of data points, and traditional visualization methods may not be able to handle such large datasets. Furthermore, big data often contains unstructured or unorganized data, making it even harder to analyze and visualize.Another challenge is that big data tends to have a larger variety of data types, such as text, images, and videos, making it harder to present the information in a coherent and visually appealing way. In addition, the speed at which big data is being generated can make it challenging to keep up with the visualizations, as old data becomes irrelevant and new data needs to be incorporated.

Techniques

To effectively visualize big data, techniques that can handle large amounts of data and different data types are essential. One such technique is data aggregation, which involves combining and summarizing the data to reveal patterns and trends. This technique helps to reduce the overwhelming amount of data into digestible insights. Another technique is data segmentation, which involves dividing the data into smaller subsets, making it more manageable to visualize. This technique is particularly useful when dealing with complex data, as it allows for a more in-depth analysis of each subset.Additionally, data visualization tools that use advanced algorithms and machine learning can automatically process and visualize big data, saving time and effort for the user. These tools can also handle different data types and produce interactive visualizations that allow for deeper exploration of the data.

Solutions

One solution to effectively visualize big data is to use interactive dashboards. These dashboards allow for real-time exploration of the data, enabling users to filter and drill down into specific subsets of data. This not only makes it easier to understand the data but also allows for more effective communication of insights to stakeholders. Another solution is to incorporate storytelling techniques into the visualization process. As big data can often be overwhelming and difficult to comprehend, presenting it in the form of a story can make it more relatable and engaging for the audience. This approach can help to create a narrative around the data and make it more memorable for the viewer. Lastly, incorporating virtual and augmented reality into the visualization of big data can provide a more immersive and engaging experience. These technologies allow users to interact with the data in a three-dimensional space, providing a new perspective on the information.

In conclusion, visualizing big data presents unique challenges that require advanced techniques and solutions. As the volume and complexity of data continue to increase, it is crucial to adapt and explore new ways to visualize and communicate this information effectively. By staying on top of the latest technologies and techniques, we can transform the overwhelming nature of big data into meaningful and actionable insights.

Chapter 15: The Power of Data Visualization in Driving Business Strategy

Data-driven decision making

In today's fast-paced business world, decisions need to be made quickly and accurately. Every minute counts, and data-driven decision making is the key to success. With the rise of big data, businesses have access to a vast amount of information, but it can be overwhelming to make sense of it all. This is where data visualization comes in. By effectively presenting data in visual form, decision-makers are able to easily analyze and understand complex information. This allows for more informed and strategic decisions to be made. Data visualization not only saves time, but it also improves the accuracy of decision making by providing a clear and comprehensive view of the data.One of the main benefits of data-driven decision making is risk mitigation. By analyzing data, businesses can identify potential risks and take proactive measures to mitigate them. This can be done through predictive analytics, which uses historical data to forecast potential risks and plan accordingly. Data visualization allows decision-makers to see patterns and trends in the data, enabling them to make informed decisions that minimize potential risks. This can be particularly beneficial for industries such as finance and insurance, where risk analysis is crucial for success.

Risk mitigation

In addition to identifying potential risks, data visualization can also help businesses mitigate them. By presenting data in a visual form, decision-makers can quickly identify areas that need improvement and take corrective measures to minimize risk. For example, a business may use data visualization to track sales trends and identify any decrease in revenue. They can then analyze the data and make necessary changes to their marketing strategy or product offerings to mitigate the risk of continued declining sales. Data visualization provides a clear and concise view of the data, making it easier to identify and address potential risks before they become serious issues.Data-driven decision making and risk mitigation are not only beneficial for businesses, but also for clients and customers. By using data to inform and guide decision-making, businesses can minimize the risk of negative outcomes for their clients. This is particularly important in industries such as healthcare, where decisions can have a significant impact on the well-being of patients. By utilizing data visualization, healthcare professionals can make more accurate and effective decisions that lead to better patient outcomes.

Identifying opportunities

Data visualization not only helps businesses protect against potential risks, but it also helps them identify new opportunities for growth. By analyzing data, businesses can identify trends and patterns that may indicate new markets or new customer needs. This can provide a competitive advantage and open up new opportunities for business growth. In today's digital landscape, data is constantly being generated and collected. For businesses to stay ahead of the curve, it is crucial to not only analyze historical data but also collect and analyze real-time data. With the help of data visualization, decision-makers can track and monitor data in real-time, allowing them to identify opportunities as they arise and take swift action. Moreover, data visualization can also aid in identifying areas for improvement within the business itself. By analyzing data from different departments and processes, decision-makers can identify bottlenecks or inefficiencies and take steps to optimize operations. This can lead to cost savings and improved overall performance.

In conclusion, data visualization is a powerful tool for driving business strategy. By providing a clear and comprehensive view of data, it enables businesses to make informed decisions, mitigate risks, and identify new opportunities. With the continuous growth of data, it is crucial for businesses to embrace data visualization in their decision-making processes in order to stay competitive in today's fast-paced and data-driven business world.

Chapter 16: Visualizing Consumer Behavior and Maximizing ROI

When it comes to successful marketing campaigns, understanding consumer behavior is key. With modern technology, there is an abundance of data and information available to marketers to help them make informed decisions. However, sifting through this massive amount of data can be overwhelming and leave marketers unsure of where to focus their efforts. This is where data visualization comes in. By using visual representations of data, marketers can gain valuable insights and make smarter decisions when it comes to targeting campaigns and measuring their return on investment (ROI).

Visualizing Consumer Behavior

Consumer behavior is influenced by a variety of factors, such as demographics, interests, and purchasing patterns. With the help of data visualization, marketers can understand these factors better and tailor their campaigns accordingly. Visualizations allow them to see trends and patterns in consumer behavior, making it easier to identify target audiences and create more effective messaging.For example, a marketing team for a clothing brand may create a visualization depicting the buying habits of their target demographic, such as age, income, and preferences. By recognizing patterns in the data, the team can then create targeted campaigns that speak directly to their ideal consumers. Without data visualization, this level of understanding would be nearly impossible to achieve.

Targeting Campaigns

Once marketers have a deeper understanding of consumer behavior, they can then use this information to target their campaigns more effectively. Data visualization allows them to see the most effective channels for reaching their target audience, such as social media, email marketing, or influencer partnerships. This helps them allocate their resources and budget more wisely, resulting in a higher ROI.Moreover, visualizations can also help in A/B testing and tracking the success of various campaigns in real-time.

This allows for quick adjustments and optimizations, saving time and resources in the long run.

Measuring ROI

Return on investment is a crucial factor for any business, and marketing is no exception. With data visualization, marketers can track the performance of their campaigns in real-time and make data-driven decisions on where to invest their resources. For example, a visualization can show the conversion rates and revenue generated by a specific campaign, allowing marketers to identify the most successful campaigns and invest more in them. Furthermore, data visualization can also help marketers see the bigger picture by connecting various data points and showing how different campaigns and strategies contribute to overall ROI. This insight can help refine future campaigns and drive even more significant returns.

In conclusion, data visualization plays a vital role in understanding consumer behavior, targeting campaigns, and measuring ROI. It allows marketers to make informed decisions, allocate resources strategically, and achieve maximum results. So, next time you dive into a new marketing campaign, remember the power of data visualization and how it can elevate your efforts to new heights.

Chapter 17: Exploring the Power of Data Visualization with Geographic Trends, Spatial Relationships, and Heatmaps

In today's data-driven world, we are constantly inundated with vast amounts of information. From social media feeds to business reports, data is all around us. But with so much data available, it can be overwhelming and challenging to make sense of it all. This is where data visualization comes in – the art of representing data in a visually appealing and easy-to-understand manner.In this chapter, we will explore how data visualization can transform complex geographical trends, spatial relationships, and heatmaps into powerful and actionable insights. We will delve into the different techniques and tools used to create these visualizations and the benefits they provide for businesses and individuals alike.

Geographic Trends

From consumer behavior to market analysis, geographical data plays a crucial role in decision-making processes. But often, this data is presented in a bland and uninteresting manner, making it difficult to grasp its significance. With data visualization, however, geographic trends can be transformed into visually stunning and informative maps. One effective technique for visualizing geographic trends is through choropleth maps. These maps use color-coding to represent different values, such as population density or sales data, in a particular area. This allows for a quick and easy comparison of data across locations. For example, a business can use a choropleth map to identify areas with the highest sales and target their marketing efforts accordingly.Another powerful visualization tool for geographic trends is the use of animated maps. With this technique, the data is presented in a time-lapse fashion, showing changes and trends over a period. This can be particularly useful in tracking the spread of a disease or understanding migration patterns.

Spatial Relationships

Understanding spatial relationships is crucial in many fields, such as urban planning, logistics, and retail. Being able to visualize the relationship between different data points can provide valuable insights into patterns and trends. This is where data visualization comes in, making it easier to understand and analyze spatial relationships. One method for visualizing spatial relationships is through the use of network diagrams. These diagrams use nodes and edges to represent connections between different data points. For example, a network diagram can help a business understand the relationship between different suppliers and how they impact supply chain efficiency.Heatmaps are another useful tool for visualizing spatial relationships. They use color-coding to represent the intensity of a particular data point in a specific area. For instance, a heat map can be used to show the areas with the most traffic congestion or customer footfall. This can help businesses optimize their routes or target their marketing efforts.

Heatmaps

Heatmaps are a popular and effective data visualization technique used to visualize data and trends in a specific area. These visualizations use color-coding to represent the intensity of a particular data point, making it easier to identify patterns and trends. One common application of heatmaps is in website analytics. By displaying the areas on a webpage where users click the most, businesses can gain insights into which parts of their website are most engaging and make necessary changes. Heatmaps can also be used in sports analytics to track player movement and identify areas of high activity. Another powerful use of heatmaps is in risk analysis. By using color-coding to represent different levels of risk in a particular area, businesses and governments can make informed decisions on resource allocation and disaster planning.In addition to traditional heatmaps, there are also more advanced versions such as hexbin maps and density maps, which provide even more precise and detailed information.

In Conclusion

Geographic trends, spatial relationships, and heatmaps are all important components of data visualization, allowing us to make sense of and act upon vast amounts of information. With the use of effective visualization techniques, businesses and individuals can gain deeper insights and improve decision-making processes. This is just one of the many ways data visualization is transforming the way we understand and interact with data. As technology continues to advance, we can expect even more sophisticated and powerful visualization techniques to emerge and revolutionize the way we use data. So, let's embrace the power of data visualization and unlock its potential for deeper insights and impactful decision-making.

Chapter 18: Storytelling With Augmented And Virtual Reality

The advancement of technology has opened up endless possibilities for data visualization and storytelling. With the rise of immersive experiences, gamification, and interactive storytelling, data can now be presented in ways that were previously unimaginable. In this chapter, we will explore the use of augmented and virtual reality in storytelling and how it can enhance the impact and reach of our data visualizations.

Immersive Experiences

Immersive experiences, also known as extended reality (XR), refer to the use of technologies such as virtual reality (VR) and augmented reality (AR) to create interactive, virtual environments. These technologies allow users to fully immerse themselves in a simulated world, blurring the lines between real and virtual. With the use of headsets, controllers, and sensors, data and storytelling can be brought to life in a whole new way. One of the key benefits of immersive experiences in data visualization is the ability to immerse the audience in the data itself. With VR, users can step into a virtual space and interact with data in a three-dimensional environment. This allows for a deeper understanding and connection to the data, as users can explore and manipulate it in real-time. For example, in a VR presentation of climate change data, users can physically move through timelines and geographies to better comprehend the impact and extent of the issue.Similarly, AR can be used to overlay data onto the real world, creating an interactive and augmented view of our surroundings. This can be particularly useful for presenting location-based data, as users can physically walk around and interact with the data in a real-world context. For instance, AR can be used to display data on historical landmarks, providing a multi-dimensional experience for visitors.

Gamification

Incorporating elements of play and game design into data visualization is known as gamification. This approach makes data more approachable and engaging, as it taps into our natural desire for competition, achievement, and discovery. Gamification can be used in both virtual and augmented reality experiences, bringing a new level of interactivity and immersion to data storytelling. A prime example of gamification in data visualization is the popular mobile game, Pokémon GO. This game uses AR to overlay virtual creatures onto the real-world environment, creating a sense of adventure and discovery for players. Likewise, data can be gamified by setting challenges, incorporating rewards, and encouraging users to explore and interact with the data in a virtual space.Furthermore, gamification can also be effective in data-driven education and training. By creating interactive and immersive experiences, users can gain a deeper understanding of complex data sets and concepts. This can be particularly valuable in industries such as healthcare, where training simulations in VR can help improve skills and decision-making in high-stress situations.

Interactive Storytelling

Interactive storytelling takes the traditional concept of storytelling to the next level, by allowing the audience to actively participate in the narrative. With the use of immersive technologies, data can be presented in a way that encourages audience engagement and interaction. This not only makes data more memorable and impactful but also allows for a more personalized and tailor-made experience for each user. Incorporating interactivity into data storytelling can also provide valuable insights into user behavior and preferences. With the use of sensors and input devices, data can be collected on how users interact with the data, which can then be used to improve future experiences. This data can also be used to personalize the experience for each user, making the storytelling more relevant and engaging.Moreover, interactive storytelling can also be used for social impact by providing a platform for underrepresented communities to tell their own stories through data. With the power of immersive experiences, marginalized voices can be amplified and their important stories and data can be shared on a global scale.

Immersive experiences, gamification, and interactive storytelling are revolutionizing the way we present and interact with data. Through the use of virtual and augmented reality, data can be transformed into immersive and interactive experiences, providing a deeper understanding and connection to the information being presented. As we continue to push the boundaries of technology, the possibilities for storytelling with data are endless.

Chapter 19: The Impact of Data Visualization on Social Change

Raising Awareness

In today's digital age, we are bombarded with an overwhelming amount of information on a daily basis. With so much noise, it can be challenging for important messages to break through and reach their intended audience. However, data visualization has proven to be a powerful tool in raising awareness about social issues and sparking conversations for change.Through the use of compelling visuals and storytelling techniques, data visualization has the ability to grab people's attention and educate them on complex social issues. Whether it is through infographics, interactive charts, or animated videos, data visualizations have the power to condense large amounts of data into easily digestible and visually appealing formats. This makes it easier for individuals to understand and spread the message to their own networks.One example of data visualization impacting social change is the #MeToo movement. The use of interactive infographics and data visualizations helped shed light on the prevalence of sexual harassment and assault, and sparked important conversations and movements for change. This shows the potential for data visualization to bring attention to social issues and drive action.

Advocating for Change

Data visualization not only has the power to raise awareness, but it can also be a powerful tool in advocating for change. By presenting data in a visual and easily accessible format, it can provide evidence and support for social causes and movements.For example, environmental organizations have used data visualization to not only raise awareness about environmental issues, but also to advocate for policy change. By presenting data on the impact of climate change in visually appealing ways, these organizations are able to make a stronger case for taking action to protect the environment.In addition, data visualization can also be used to track progress and measure the impact of initiatives and advocacy efforts. This allows organizations to showcase the effectiveness of their work and rally support for continued change.

Engaging Communities

One of the key elements of successful social change is community engagement. When individuals feel connected and involved in a cause, they are more likely to take action and support the change. Data visualization has the power to engage communities in new and innovative ways.Social media platforms have become a powerful medium for sharing data visualizations and spreading awareness and support for social causes. By creating visually appealing and shareable content, organizations and individuals can engage their communities and build a movement for change.Furthermore, data visualization also has the potential to engage communities offline. With the help of augmented or virtual reality, data can be brought to life and individuals can have a more immersive experience with the data. This can create a stronger emotional connection and inspire individuals to take action.

The Role of Data Visualization in Social Impact

In conclusion, data visualization plays a crucial role in raising awareness, advocating for change, and engaging communities in social impact efforts. Its ability to convey complex information in a visually appealing and easily understandable format makes it a powerful tool for creating actionable insights and driving social change. As we continue to evolve in the digital world, data visualization will undoubtedly play a significant role in promoting social progress and creating a better future for all.

Chapter 20: The Future of Data Visualization

Data visualization has long been a powerful tool for turning complex data into actionable insights. With advancements in technology and the increasing demand for data-driven decision-making, the field of data visualization is constantly evolving. In this chapter, we will explore the emerging trends, technological advancements, and predictions for the future of data visualization.

Emerging Trends

As data becomes more abundant and accessible, the demand for data visualization tools and techniques is also increasing. One of the emerging trends in data visualization is the use of augmented and virtual reality. With the help of these technologies, data can be visualized in a more immersive and interactive way, providing a new level of understanding and engagement for the audience. Another trend in data visualization is the integration of storytelling techniques. Instead of solely relying on charts and graphs, data is now being presented in a narrative form, making it more relatable and captivating for the audience. This trend also highlights the importance of considering the audience and tailoring the message accordingly. Furthermore, there is a growing trend in incorporating emotions into data visualizations. By incorporating colors, images, and other design elements, data can evoke a more emotional response from the audience, leading to a deeper understanding and connection with the data.

Technological Advancements

The rapid advancements in technology have greatly enhanced the capabilities of data visualization. Machine learning, artificial intelligence, and natural language processing are just a few of the technologies being used to analyze and visualize large and complex datasets. These advancements allow for more sophisticated and accurate visualizations, providing deeper insights into the data.Cloud computing has also played a significant role in the evolution of data visualization. With the help of cloud-based tools and platforms, data can be analyzed and visualized in real-time, increasing the speed and efficiency of the process. This has made data visualization more accessible to individuals and organizations of all sizes.

Predictions

As we look into the future of data visualization, it is clear that it will continue to evolve and transform. One prediction is that data visualization will become more personalized. With the help of artificial intelligence and machine learning, visualizations will be tailored to the individual needs and preferences of the audience. Another prediction is the use of data visualization for real-time decision-making. With the advancements in technology and the availability of real-time data, visualizations will be used to make quick and informed decisions. This will have a significant impact on industries such as finance, healthcare, and logistics. Furthermore, the use of data visualization in virtual reality is expected to become more prominent. With the help of VR, data can be visualized in a three-dimensional space, providing a more immersive and interactive experience for the audience.

In conclusion, the future of data visualization is bright and full of possibilities. With emerging trends, technological advancements, and predictions, we can see that data visualization will continue to play a crucial role in understanding and utilizing data in a meaningful way. As technology advances and new innovations are introduced, it is essential for us to adapt and stay ahead of the curve to fully harness the power of data visualization.

Chapter 21: Overcoming Common Challenges in Data Visualization

Data visualization has become an essential tool in today's data-driven world. With an overwhelming abundance of data available to us, it has become more important than ever to present this data in a meaningful and understandable way. However, as with any new technology, there are challenges that come along with it. In this chapter, we will explore some common challenges that organizations face when it comes to implementing data visualization and how to overcome them.

Data overload

One of the biggest challenges in data visualization is dealing with data overload. We are constantly bombarded with an enormous amount of data from various sources, making it difficult to sort through and make sense of it all. This overload of data can be overwhelming and can hinder our ability to make informed decisions. To overcome this challenge, it is important to first understand what data is important and relevant to our goals. It is crucial to have a clear understanding of our objectives and the questions we are trying to answer with the data. This helps us filter out unnecessary data and focus on what matters most. Additionally, using data visualization tools that allow for easy filtering and sorting can help us manage the overwhelming amount of data more effectively.Another approach to dealing with data overload is to prioritize. Instead of trying to visualize all the data at once, focus on the key data points that will provide the most valuable insights. This not only helps in managing the overwhelming data but also ensures that we are presenting the most relevant information to our audience.

Lack of resources

Implementing data visualization can also be challenging due to a lack of resources. Data visualization requires a combination of skills and tools, and not all organizations have the necessary resources to invest in this technology. Many may not have a dedicated team or the budget to invest in expensive visualization tools. One way to overcome this challenge is by leveraging open-source and free data visualization tools available. These tools are constantly improving and can provide a cost-effective solution for organizations with limited resources. Additionally, organizations can also train their existing employees in data visualization skills to create a dedicated team within the organization.Collaboration can also help overcome the challenge of a lack of resources. By partnering with other organizations or experts in the field, resources can be shared, and costs can be reduced. This also brings in diverse perspectives and skill sets, leading to more effective data visualization.

Resistance to change

Change is never easy, and this holds true for implementing data visualization as well. Organizations may face resistance from employees who are not familiar with the technology or are hesitant to adapt to new ways of presenting data. This can create roadblocks in the implementation and success of data visualization. To overcome resistance to change, it is important to involve all stakeholders from the beginning. This includes training and educating employees on the benefits of data visualization and the role it plays in decision-making. It is also crucial to communicate the importance and impact of data visualization in achieving organizational goals. Another approach is to start small and gradually scale up. Begin with simple visualizations of data that will immediately showcase the value of this technology. This will help build trust and confidence in employees, making it easier for them to embrace change.

In conclusion, data visualization is a powerful tool that can help organizations make informed decisions and drive growth. However, it is not without its challenges. By understanding and addressing the challenges of data overload, lack of resources, and resistance to change, organizations can successfully implement and leverage data visualization to their advantage. Remember, it is important to have a clear understanding of your goals, prioritize, collaborate, and involve all stakeholders to ensure the success of data visualization.

Chapter 22: Collaborating with Data Professionals for Enhanced Visualizations

Data visualization is an art form that requires both technical skills and creativity. As a non-data professional, collaborating with experts in the field can take your visualizations to the next level. By working with data professionals, you can tap into their expertise and gain a deeper understanding of the data, leading to more insightful and effective visualizations.

Collaborating with Data Professionals

When it comes to data visualization, it's important to recognize your own limitations and seek collaboration with those who have the necessary skills and knowledge. Data professionals have a deep understanding of data, including how to collect, clean, analyze, and interpret it. By collaborating with them, you can ensure that your visualizations are based on accurate and relevant data. Additionally, data professionals can bring a fresh perspective to your visualizations. They can help you identify patterns and insights that you may have missed and provide valuable feedback on the effectiveness of your visuals. Collaborating with data professionals can also save you time and resources, as they are experts in handling and analyzing large datasets.When working with data professionals, clear communication is key. Clearly articulate your goals and objectives for the visualization, and be open to their suggestions and insights. By fostering a collaborative and open-minded environment, you can create a strong partnership that will lead to visually stunning and impactful data visualizations.

Using Storytelling Tools to Enhance Data Visualization

Storytelling is an essential element of effective data visualization. Combining data with a compelling narrative can make complex information more accessible and engaging for your audience. Working with data professionals can help you harness the power of storytelling and take your visualizations to the next level. Data professionals have a wealth of knowledge about different storytelling techniques and tools. They can help you identify the best approach for your visualization and guide you through the storytelling process. Whether it's through incorporating narrative elements, using characters to represent data, or creating an interactive story, data professionals can help you build a captivating and impactful data visualization.In addition, data professionals can introduce you to various visualization tools and platforms that can enhance your storytelling. These tools can help you create dynamic and interactive visuals that will captivate your audience and bring your data to life.

Fostering Creativity in Data Visualization

Collaborating with data professionals not only provides technical support, but also fosters creativity. Data professionals can help you think outside the box and explore unconventional ways of presenting data. They can introduce you to new visualization techniques and tools, challenging you to think beyond traditional charts and graphs. Furthermore, working with data professionals can help alleviate the pressure and stress associated with data visualization. As a non-expert, it can be overwhelming to handle and analyze large datasets on your own. By working with data professionals, you can focus on the creative aspects of visualization, such as designing and implementing an engaging narrative, while they handle the technical aspects. Just as artists collaborate and bounce ideas off each other, collaborating with data professionals can spark new ideas and inspire innovative data visualizations. By combining your unique perspectives and expertise, you can create visualizations that are truly one-of-a-kind.

In conclusion, collaborating with data professionals is essential for creating impactful and effective data visualizations. They bring a wealth of technical knowledge and creativity to the table, helping you craft visually stunning and compelling narratives. By fostering a collaborative and open-minded relationship with data professionals, you can take your visualizations to new heights. So don't be afraid to seek collaboration and embrace the power of teamwork in data visualization.

Chapter 23: Enhancing Visualizations with Data Storytellers

Data visualization has become an essential tool in today's business world, with its ability to transform complex data into easily understandable visuals. However, what makes a data visualization truly impactful and memorable is not just its aesthetics, but the story that it tells. This is where data storytellers come in – experts who can use data to create dynamic visuals and weave them into compelling narratives. In this chapter, we will explore the art and science of using data storytelling through dynamic visuals and multimedia to create engaging and immersive presentations.

Dynamic visuals

Gone are the days when data was presented in dull and static charts and graphs. With advancements in technology, data visualization has evolved into a dynamic and interactive experience, making it more engaging and effective. Dynamic visuals are not just aesthetically pleasing but also allow for better analysis and understanding of data, as they can be manipulated and customized in real-time. From animated charts and graphs to interactive dashboards, the possibilities are endless.But creating dynamic visuals is not just about adding flashy effects or animations. It requires a deep understanding of the data and the message that needs to be conveyed. A skilled data storyteller knows how to use the right visual elements to highlight the key insights and guide the audience towards the desired conclusion. Whether it is a line graph, a pie chart, or a heat map, each visual element must have a purpose and contribute to the overall story.

Storytelling through multimedia

While data visualization is a powerful tool on its own, when combined with multimedia elements such as videos, images, and audio, it becomes even more impactful. Data storytelling through multimedia can evoke emotions, create a personal connection with the audience, and make the information more memorable. For instance, a data visualization about the impact of climate change can be accompanied by a video showcasing real-life stories of individuals affected by it. This adds depth and authenticity to the narrative, making it more compelling.With the rise of social media and other digital platforms, data storytelling through multimedia has become even more prevalent. It allows for the information to reach a wider audience and resonate with them on a deeper level. Data journalists and digital content creators have mastered the art of using multimedia to tell compelling stories that drive action and change.

Creating engaging presentations

The purpose of data visualization is not just to present information but to communicate it effectively to the target audience. And creating an engaging presentation is crucial to achieving this goal. A data storyteller knows how to structure the data into a narrative that captivates the audience's attention and keeps them engaged throughout the presentation. One of the key elements of an engaging data-driven presentation is a clear and concise story arc. This means having a compelling beginning that hooks the audience, a middle that presents the data in a logical and easy-to-follow way, and an impactful ending that leaves a lasting impression. A data storyteller also knows how to leverage different multimedia elements, design principles, and storytelling techniques to create a visually appealing and engaging presentation. Moreover, an engaging presentation not only conveys information but also leaves room for the audience to interact and participate. This can be achieved through interactive elements such as polls, quizzes, or Q&A sessions. It not only makes the presentation more dynamic but also allows for a deeper understanding and involvement from the audience.

In conclusion, data storytelling through dynamic visuals and multimedia is an art that requires a perfect blend of creativity, technical skills, and data analysis. By mastering this art, data storytellers can create engaging and impactful presentations that not only convey information but also inspire action and change. So, whether you are a data analyst, a marketer, or a business professional, learning the art of data storytelling can take your data visualization skills to the next level and make your presentations truly unforgettable.

Chapter 24: Visualizing Learning: Enhancing Education through Data Visualization

Data visualization has become an increasingly important tool in education, as it allows students to better understand complex concepts and information. By transforming data into visually appealing and interactive forms, students are able to engage with the content in a more meaningful way and can actively participate in their own learning journey. In this chapter, we will explore the various ways in which data visualization is being used to enhance education, including visualizing learning concepts, interactive learning tools, and the growing trend of gamification in the education sector.

Visualizing Learning Concepts

In traditional education, students are often presented with large amounts of information in the form of textbooks, lectures, and worksheets. While these methods are still common, they often fail to capture the attention of students and can make learning feel like a mundane and repetitive task. However, with the use of data visualization, educators are able to transform this overwhelming information into visually appealing and engaging formats.Through the use of charts, graphs, and infographics, students can see and understand relationships between different concepts and data points. For example, a visual representation of the water cycle can help students understand the flow and transformation of water on Earth in a more tangible way than simply reading about it. By incorporating visual aids in the learning process, students are able to grasp complex concepts more easily and retain the information for a longer period of time.

Interactive Learning Tools

The use of interactive learning tools has revolutionized the way students engage with education. Instead of being passive recipients of information, students are now actively involved in the learning process. Data visualization has played a key role in this shift, as it allows for the creation of interactive learning tools that encourage students to explore and manipulate data on their own.For instance, interactive maps and timelines can enable students to examine historical events from multiple angles and gather insights that they may not have otherwise. In science classes, students can explore the human body through interactive diagrams and videos, making the learning experience more immersive and engaging. These tools not only help students understand the subject matter more deeply, but also develop critical thinking and problem-solving skills.

Gamification in Education

One of the most exciting developments in data visualization in education is its integration with gamification. Gamification is the use of gaming principles and mechanics, such as points, levels, and rewards, in non-gaming contexts. In education, this means incorporating elements of gameplay into the learning process to make it more enjoyable and engaging for students.Data visualization plays a crucial role in gamification by providing students with visual feedback on their progress and achievements. For example, a progress bar can show students how much they have accomplished and how much is left to complete a task. This visual feedback system motivates students to continue learning and achieving their goals. In addition, data visualization can also be used to create game-like scenarios, making the learning process more fun and interactive.

Conclusion

Data visualization has transformed the landscape of education, making it more engaging, interactive, and effective for students. By visualizing learning concepts, creating interactive learning tools, and incorporating gamification, educators are able to enhance the learning experience and empower students to take charge of their own education. As the technology behind data visualization continues to advance, we can only expect to see more exciting and innovative applications in the field of education, making learning a more enjoyable and fruitful experience for students.

Chapter 25: Data Visualization Across Cultures

Cultural Sensitivity

When it comes to data visualization, it's important to keep in mind that different cultures may have different ways of interpreting and communicating data. As creators of data visualizations, we have a responsibility to be culturally sensitive and aware of the impact our visualizations may have on different audiences. One key aspect of cultural sensitivity in data visualization is understanding cultural norms and values. For example, some cultures may value individualism and prefer visualizations that highlight individual data points, while others may value collectivism and prefer visualizations that show trends and patterns within a group. It's important to research and understand the cultural context in which your visualizations will be presented.Another consideration is to avoid any unintentional biases or stereotypes in your visualizations. Data often reflects societal biases, but as data visualizers, we must strive to present it in an unbiased and objective manner. This means being mindful of any cultural or demographic biases in your data and making efforts to present the information in an accurate and fair way. Cultural sensitivity also involves understanding the visual language and symbols used in different cultures. For example, certain colors may have different meanings in different cultures. Red, which is often associated with power and passion in Western cultures, may symbolize happiness and good fortune in Chinese cultures. It's important to be conscious of these differences when creating data visualizations for different audiences.

Design Considerations

When designing data visualizations for different cultures, there are several design considerations to keep in mind. One important aspect is the use of language. If your visualization will be presented to a non-English speaking audience, it's important to translate labels and text into their native language. This not only makes the information more accessible, but it also shows an effort to cater to their specific cultural background.Another design consideration is the use of symbols and visuals. As mentioned earlier, certain symbols may have different meanings in different cultures. It's important to research and understand the symbolism behind the visuals used in your visualizations to avoid any cultural misunderstandings.

In addition, the use of visuals in data visualizations can also vary across cultures. Some cultures may prefer minimalist design with simple charts and graphs, while others may prefer more intricate and decorative visualizations. It's important to consider the visual preferences of your audience and adapt your designs accordingly.

International Best Practices

As data visualization becomes a global practice, there are a few best practices that have emerged for creating visualizations that are culturally sensitive and effective. One key practice is to involve diverse perspectives and voices in the creation process. This can help to identify any cultural biases or misunderstandings and ensure the visualization is inclusive and informative for all audiences.Another important practice is to test and iterate the visualization with members of the target audience. This can help identify any issues or concerns before the final visualization is presented. It also shows a commitment to understanding and meeting the needs of the audience. Keeping up with global trends and approaches in data visualization is also essential. As cultures and technologies evolve, so do the ways in which information is communicated and interpreted. Reading case studies and attending conferences or workshops focused on data visualization can help broaden your understanding and keep your visualizations relevant and effective in a global context.Data visualization may seem like a universal language, but in reality, it can be influenced by cultural factors and preferences. As responsible and mindful data visualizers, it's important to consider cultural sensitivity, design considerations, and international best practices when creating visualizations for diverse audiences. By doing so, we can ensure our visualizations are impactful and inclusive, no matter where they are being presented.

Chapter 26: Choosing the Best Representation for Your Data Visualization

Data is everywhere, and with the advancement of technology, we now have access to vast amounts of it. However, to truly gain insights from this data, it must be presented in a visually appealing and organized manner. This is where data visualization comes in – the art and science of representing data in a way that is easy to understand and interpret. In chapter 26, we will explore the different types of data visualization techniques and discuss the key factors to consider when choosing the best representation for your data.

Bar Charts vs. Line Graphs

When it comes to displaying categorical data, two commonly used methods are bar charts and line graphs. Bar charts are useful for comparing data between different categories, where each bar represents a category and the height of the bar indicates the value. On the other hand, line graphs are ideal for showing the trend of data over time, with each point on the line indicating a specific data point.The key to choosing between these two representations lies in the goal of your visualization. If you want to highlight differences between categories, a bar chart would be the most effective option. However, if the focus is on displaying trends or patterns over time, a line graph would be more suitable. It is also important to consider the complexity of your data – if there are too many data points, a line graph can become cluttered and difficult to interpret, whereas a bar chart would be able to handle more data points without losing its visual appeal.

Scatter Plots vs. Heatmaps

When dealing with numerical data, two types of visualizations that are commonly used are scatter plots and heatmaps. Scatter plots are useful for identifying the relationship between two variables, as each data point is represented as a dot on the graph. The position of the dot indicates the values of the two variables, and patterns in the data can be easily identified. On the other hand, heatmaps use color to represent data values, with darker colors indicating higher values and lighter colors indicating lower values. They are efficient in displaying large datasets and identifying patterns or clusters within the data. Heatmaps are particularly useful for geographical data, as they provide a clear visual representation of data distribution across a map.The choice between these two types of visuals depends on the purpose of your visualization. If the goal is to identify relationships and patterns between two variables, a scatter plot would be the most effective option. However, if the focus is on displaying a large dataset and identifying trends or clusters, a heatmap would be more suitable.

Choosing the Best Representation

When it comes to choosing the best representation for your data, there are a few key factors to consider. The first is the type of data you are working with – is it categorical or numerical? This will determine whether a bar chart or a scatter plot would be more appropriate. The next factor to consider is the purpose of your visualization – are you trying to identify relationships, trends, or patterns? This will guide you towards a specific type of visualization, such as a line graph or a heatmap. Another important factor is the complexity of your data. If it is a large dataset with many data points, you may need a visual that can handle a high volume of data without becoming cluttered and difficult to interpret. In this case, a heatmap or a bar chart with grouped bars would be more suitable. Additionally, it is crucial to keep in mind the audience for your visualization – will it be a technical audience or a non-technical one? This will influence the level of complexity and detail in your visualization. Lastly, it is essential to experiment with different types of visualizations before finalizing your choice. By trying out different options, you can determine which representation best showcases your data and helps you convey your message effectively.

In conclusion, choosing the right representation for your data visualization is crucial in delivering actionable insights. By understanding the different types of visualizations and considering key factors such as the type of data, purpose, complexity, and audience, you can create a visually appealing and informative representation of your data. Remember to always experiment with different options and choose the representation that best suits the goals and needs of your data visualization.

Chapter 27: Forecasting Future Insights with Predictive Data Visualization

From predicting consumer behavior to anticipating market trends, data visualization has become an essential tool for forecasting future insights. As the world becomes more data-driven, businesses and organizations are turning to predictive modeling techniques to stay ahead of the game. In this chapter, we will explore how data visualization can enhance the forecasting process, from creating accurate models to effectively interpreting and communicating insights.

Forecasting Trends

The business landscape is constantly changing, and keeping up with the latest trends is crucial for success. While traditional forecasting methods rely on historical data to predict future outcomes, data visualization allows us to analyze real-time information and identify patterns and trends that might not be apparent through a traditional approach. Through visual storytelling, data can be transformed into a powerful tool for forecasting trends. By visualizing large datasets in a simple and intuitive way, we can identify patterns and outliers that can help forecast future trends. Data visualization also allows for the incorporation of external factors such as demographic shifts, technological advancements, and economic changes that can impact trends.With the use of interactive visualizations, we can also examine different scenarios and make adjustments to our forecasts in real-time. This dynamic approach to forecasting allows for a more agile and accurate prediction of future trends.

Predictive Modeling

Predictive modeling is a statistical technique that uses historical data to predict future outcomes. By identifying and analyzing patterns in past data, predictive models can be used to anticipate future events and behavior with a certain degree of accuracy. However, the effectiveness of these models relies heavily on the interpretation of data.This is where data visualization plays a crucial role. By transforming complex data into visual representations, predictive models become easier to interpret and communicate to stakeholders. With the use of interactive visualizations, we can also adjust variables and parameters in real-time to test different scenarios and fine-tune our models for more accurate predictions.

Interpretation and Communication of Insights

The success of a predictive model depends not only on its accuracy but also on the communication of its insights to different stakeholders. Even the most accurate and insightful predictions can be lost in a sea of numbers and jargon without proper visualization. Data visualization allows for easy interpretation and communication of insights to different audiences, regardless of their technical knowledge. With the use of compelling visual storytelling, we can engage stakeholders and effectively communicate potential future outcomes. Interactive visualizations also enable stakeholders to explore and analyze the data themselves, promoting a deeper understanding and acceptance of the insights. Furthermore, incorporating visualizations into presentations and reports can make them more engaging, memorable, and impactful. It allows stakeholders to see the bigger picture, identify critical patterns and trends, and understand the implications of the forecasted insights.

In conclusion, the combination of predictive modeling and data visualization provides a powerful tool for forecasting future insights. With its ability to identify patterns and trends, adjust parameters and variables, and effectively communicate insights to diverse audiences, data visualization truly enhances the forecasting process. As technology continues to advance and data becomes more abundant, the importance of data visualization in forecasting trends will only continue to grow. So, embrace the power of data visualization and get ready to forecast the future with confidence.

Chapter 28: Creating Actionable Insights with Data Visualization and Storytelling

Usability Testing: Improving User Experience with Data Visualization

Usability testing is an essential step in the design and development process of any data visualization. It involves evaluating the design and functionality of a visualization by testing it with real users. By observing how users interact with the visualization and gathering feedback, designers can identify any usability issues and make necessary improvements before the final product is released. The goal of usability testing is to ensure that the data visualization is intuitive, easy to navigate, and provides a positive user experience. This is especially important in the rapidly evolving world of data visualization, where new tools and techniques are constantly emerging. By understanding how users interact with data visualizations, designers can adapt and improve their techniques to meet the changing needs of their audience.During usability testing, user-centered design principles should be followed to ensure that the visualization meets the needs and expectations of the target audience. This approach involves understanding the user's goals, tasks, and preferences, and designing with them in mind. By putting the user at the center of the design process, designers can create data visualizations that are both practical and aesthetically pleasing.

User-Centered Design: Putting the User First

User-centered design (UCD) is a design approach that involves understanding the needs and preferences of the users and designing with them in mind. It is a human-focused design approach that aims to create products that are intuitive, easy to use, and enjoyable for the end-user. In the context of data visualization, user-centered design is crucial in ensuring that the visualization is effective in delivering insights and engaging the audience.One key aspect of UCD is the use of personas, which are fictional representations of the target users. By creating personas, designers can better understand the needs and preferences of their audience and design accordingly. This approach also involves iterative testing and refinement, where prototypes are continuously evaluated and improved based on user feedback.

Information Architecture: Building a Solid Foundation for Effective Data Visualization

Information architecture is the practice of organizing and structuring information in a way that is easy to understand and navigate. In the context of data visualization, information architecture is crucial in creating a solid foundation for delivering actionable insights. It involves understanding the data and its relationships, and designing a structure that makes sense for the target audience.When creating a data visualization, designers must carefully consider the information architecture to ensure that the visualization is both visually appealing and easy to understand. This involves organizing the data in a logical way, using clear labels and visual cues, and providing contextual information to help users understand the data. By carefully planning the information architecture, designers can create a data visualization that is intuitive and efficient in delivering insights to the audience.

The Importance of User-Centered Usability Testing in Information Architecture

Usability testing and user-centered design are both crucial elements for creating an effective information architecture. By incorporating these principles, designers can ensure that the data visualization is user-friendly and meets the needs and expectations of the target audience. During the usability testing phase, designers can evaluate the effectiveness of the information architecture by observing how users interact with the visualization. This feedback can then be used to make necessary improvements to the architecture, such as rearranging or grouping data in a more intuitive way.Furthermore, user-centered design principles should be applied throughout the information architecture process. This involves understanding the user's information needs and designing the structure and layout of the visualization accordingly. By keeping the user at the center of the design process, designers can create a data visualization that effectively presents insights and engages the audience.

The Evolving Landscape of Usability Testing, User-Centered Design, and Information Architecture

As the field of data visualization continues to evolve, so do the practices of usability testing, user-centered design, and information architecture. With the introduction of new technology and tools, designers must adapt and improve their techniques to meet the changing needs of their audience. In recent years, the importance of UX (user experience) design has become increasingly recognized in the field of data visualization. UX design focuses on creating a positive and enjoyable experience for the user, and encompasses principles from usability testing and user-centered design. As data visualizations become more interactive and complex, UX design will play a crucial role in creating a seamless and engaging user experience.Additionally, with the rise of big data and the increasing demand for data-driven decision making, the role of information architecture in data visualization is becoming even more crucial. Designers must find ways to effectively organize and present large and complex data sets in a way that is both visually appealing and easy to understand.

Conclusion

Usability testing, user-centered design, and information architecture are all essential components of creating actionable insights with data visualization and storytelling. By incorporating these principles into the design process, designers can ensure that their data visualizations are effective in delivering insights and engaging the audience. As technology and data continue to evolve, these practices will play an even more significant role in creating impactful and meaningful data visualizations.

Chapter 29: Data Visualization in Journalism and Media

Storytelling is a powerful art that has been around for centuries. It captivates us, transports us to different worlds, and helps us make sense of the world around us. Thanks to advancements in technology, we now have the ability to enhance our stories with data visualization. In this chapter, we will explore the dynamic relationship between data visualization and storytelling in journalism and media.

Storytelling through data

In the ever-changing landscape of media and journalism, storytelling remains a vital element, and data visualization has become an integral tool in amplifying the impact of these stories. By incorporating data into their narratives, journalists and media professionals can provide a deeper understanding of complex issues and convey a more compelling message. The use of data visualization in storytelling is not limited to just traditional media outlets. With the rise of social media, citizen journalism has also emerged as a powerful force. Individuals can now use data visualization tools to create their own visual stories, giving them a platform to share their perspectives and amplify their message.One prime example of data visualization used in storytelling is The New York Times' interactive article, "Snowfall: The Avalanche at Tunnel Creek." The piece combined gripping storytelling with stunning visuals, including interactive maps and videos, to tell the tragic story of an avalanche and its impact on the skiers caught in its path. This groundbreaking article set a new standard for multimedia storytelling in the digital age.

Visualizing news stories

The role of data visualization in journalism extends beyond feature articles and investigations. It is also a crucial component in delivering news stories to audiences. With the 24-hour news cycle, journalists are under immense pressure to present complex information in a quick and digestible format. Data visualization allows them to simplify and clarify information, making it more accessible to the general public.News organizations have also been using data visualization to enhance their coverage of events and breaking news. During the 2016 US presidential election, the New York Times created a live visualization of election results, providing real-time updates and insightful analysis. This allowed readers to engage with the data and better understand the election process.

Ethics and accuracy in data journalism

As with any form of journalism, ethics and accuracy are crucial in data journalism. The use of data can make stories more persuasive, but it also requires a higher level of responsibility. With the potential to influence public opinion, journalists must ensure that their data sources are credible and that their visualizations accurately reflect the data. Data visualization created for journalistic purposes should be unbiased and transparent. It is essential to provide readers with the context and limitations of the data to avoid misleading them. Journalists also need to be aware of the potential consequences of their visualizations and ensure they do not reinforce harmful stereotypes or perpetuate misinformation.In 2019, the Washington Post came under scrutiny for an article that used inaccurate data to show how many children were separated from their families at the US-Mexico border. The article was later retracted and an editor's note was issued, reiterating the importance of accuracy in data journalism.

Conclusion

Data visualization has transformed the way we consume stories from the media. By incorporating data into narratives, journalists can not only make their stories more engaging but also provide a better understanding of complex issues. As technology continues to advance, we can only expect to see more innovative uses of data visualization in journalism and media. However, with this power comes a great responsibility to uphold ethics and accuracy, ensuring that the stories told are informative and truthful.

Chapter 30: Data Visualization for Internal Communications

Data-driven decision making

In today's fast-paced business world, data is king. It is the driving force behind decision making in every industry and plays a crucial role in the success of any company. However, raw data alone is not enough to guide effective decision making – it must be presented in a way that is easily understood and actionable. This is where data visualization comes into play. Data visualization is the process of transforming complex data into visually appealing and easily understandable charts, graphs, and infographics. It allows companies to make sense of vast amounts of information and identify patterns and trends that may not have been apparent before. By visualizing data, decision makers can quickly and accurately assess the current state of their company, identify areas for improvement, and make informed decisions that lead to success.Not only does data visualization aid in decision making, but it has also become a vital tool for communication within organizations.

Communicating company insights

In today's digital age, businesses are inundated with vast amounts of data from various sources. However, all this data is useless if it cannot be effectively communicated to the relevant stakeholders. This is where data visualization shines – it translates complex data into easily digestible visuals that convey important insights and information. Data visualization can help communicate company insights in a variety of ways. For instance, employees can use interactive dashboards to track their performance and compare it to company goals and benchmarks. This allows for a more transparent and collaborative environment, where employees can take ownership of their work and make data-driven decisions.Additionally, data visualization is a powerful tool for communicating company updates, financial performance, and strategies. Instead of presenting dry numbers and statistics, data visualizations can tell a story and engage the audience emotionally. As a result, employees are more likely to understand and remember the information presented to them, leading to better decision making and alignment with company goals.

Employee engagement

Effective communication is essential in maintaining a motivated and engaged workforce. Data visualization can go a long way in boosting employee engagement and creating a culture of transparency and accountability within an organization. By making data accessible and understandable, employees can have a better understanding of their role in the company and see how their contributions impact business outcomes. Data visualizations can also be used to recognize and reward top-performing employees, providing a sense of accomplishment and motivation to continue excelling. Additionally, employee engagement surveys can be presented in a visual format, allowing for easier analysis and identification of areas for improvement.Incorporating data visualization into internal communications can foster a data-driven culture where employees are empowered to make decisions and contribute to the success of the company.

Data visualization has become an essential tool for data-driven decision making and effective communication within organizations. By transforming complex data into visually appealing and easily understandable visuals, data visualization enables businesses to make informed decisions, communicate company insights, and boost employee engagement. As technology and data continue to evolve, the role of data visualization in internal communications will only become more crucial in driving the success of businesses.

Chapter 31: Data Visualization for Predictive Analytics

Predictive analytics, a term that may sound daunting to some, is actually a powerful tool that allows us to analyze data and make informed predictions about future outcomes. With the help of data visualization, this process becomes even more effective and efficient. In this chapter, we will explore how data visualization can be used to automate insights, identify patterns, and predict outcomes.

Automating Insights

Gone are the days when data analysis required hours of manual work. With the advancement of technology, we now have the capability to automate insights and extract valuable information from large data sets in a matter of minutes. This is where data visualization comes into play. By using data visualization tools, we can analyze complex data and instantly identify key insights. The visual representation of data allows us to quickly make connections and draw conclusions that may have otherwise been overlooked. Data visualization also helps us to identify data outliers and anomalies that can provide valuable insights into the data set.Moreover, automated data visualization can also identify patterns and trends in data that may not be as evident to the human eye. This enables us to gain a deeper understanding of the data and make more accurate predictions.

Identifying Patterns

One of the primary purposes of data visualization is to identify patterns and trends in data. By displaying data in a visual format, it becomes easier to spot recurring patterns and understand the relationships between different variables. For example, by creating a line graph of sales data over a period of time, we can quickly identify any seasonal trends or spikes in sales. This information can then be used to make predictions about future sales for various time periods.Data visualization can also help us identify patterns in customer behavior, which can be crucial for businesses. By analyzing customer data, such as purchase history, website interactions, and social media engagement, we can gain valuable insights into customer preferences, buying habits, and potential future behavior. This information can then be used to create targeted marketing campaigns and improve overall business strategy.

Predicting Outcomes

Data visualization plays an essential role in predictive analytics by helping us to make informed predictions about future outcomes. By analyzing past data and identifying patterns and trends, we can use data visualization to make accurate predictions about what may happen in the future. For businesses, predictive analytics can be used to forecast sales, customer behavior and identify potential risks and opportunities. By visualizing this data, business leaders can make strategic decisions and plan for the future with more confidence. In other fields, such as healthcare, data visualization can be used to predict the likelihood of certain diseases, monitor patient progress, and make informed decisions about treatment plans. This can ultimately lead to more effective and personalized care for patients. Data visualization can also be used to predict outcomes in the field of sports. By analyzing data such as player statistics, game footage, and weather conditions, coaches can make data-driven decisions about the players' training schedules and game strategies. This can potentially lead to better performance and more successful outcomes for the team.

In conclusion, data visualization is a powerful tool for predictive analytics, enabling us to automate insights, identify patterns, and predict outcomes. As the field of data science continues to evolve, we can expect to see even more sophisticated and accurate forms of data visualization that will help us make more informed and precise predictions. By using data visualization in conjunction with other analytical techniques, we can unlock a wealth of insights and drive positive change in various industries.

Chapter 32: Visualizing Data for Health and Wellness

In today's world, where technology and data are ubiquitous, we have access to vast amounts of information about our health and wellness. From fitness trackers and smartwatches to online health portals, we are constantly monitoring and tracking our physical and mental well-being. However, the challenge lies in understanding and making sense of this data to improve our overall health.

Monitoring Health Trends

Thanks to advancements in technology, we now have the ability to monitor various health trends and track changes over time. This can range from tracking our daily step count to monitoring our heart rate and sleep patterns. With the help of data visualization, we can gain a deeper understanding of these trends and patterns. For instance, visualizing our daily step count over a period of time can help us identify trends in our physical activity. Are there certain days of the week where we tend to be more active or less active? Are there any patterns in our step count that can be attributed to external factors such as weather or work schedules? By tracking and visualizing this data, we can adjust our daily routine and make healthier choices.Another example is visualizing our sleep patterns. By monitoring our sleep quality and duration and visualizing the data, we can identify any underlying issues that may be affecting our sleep. Perhaps we are not getting enough restful sleep or we may have a specific sleep disorder that needs to be addressed. With the help of data visualization, we can pinpoint these issues and take steps towards improving our sleep and overall well-being.

Identifying Risk Factors

In addition to monitoring trends, data visualization can also help us identify potential risk factors for various health conditions. By analyzing and visualizing our health data, we can gain valuable insights into our own health and identify potential red flags that may require further attention. For example, if we regularly track our blood pressure levels and visualize the data, we can easily spot any abnormal spikes or dips in our readings. This can be an early warning sign of hypertension or other cardiovascular issues, allowing us to take preventative measures before it becomes a serious health concern.Similarly, tracking and visualizing our weight, cholesterol levels, and other key health metrics can also help identify risk factors for conditions like obesity, diabetes, and heart disease. By regularly monitoring and visualizing our health data, we can proactively manage our health and make necessary lifestyle changes to prevent and manage these conditions.

Communicating Health Information

Data visualization is not only beneficial for individuals but also for healthcare professionals and organizations. By using data visualization, healthcare providers can better communicate important health information to their patients. Visual representations of data can help patients better understand their health conditions and treatment plans. For instance, visualizing the effects of smoking on the lungs can be a powerful tool to encourage smokers to quit. Similarly, visualizing the outcomes of a specific treatment plan can help patients understand the potential benefits and make informed decisions about their health. Data visualization can also be used to communicate health information on a larger scale. Healthcare organizations and public health agencies can use visualizations to communicate important public health messages, such as promoting healthy eating habits or highlighting the impacts of pollution on our health. By presenting data in a visually appealing and easy-to-understand manner, organizations can effectively raise awareness and drive positive change in the community.

In conclusion, data visualization is a powerful tool in the field of health and wellness. By monitoring health trends, identifying risk factors, and communicating health information, we can use data visualization to improve our overall health and well-being. With the ever-growing availability of health data, data visualization will continue to play a crucial role in empowering individuals to take control of their health and make informed decisions about their well-being.

Chapter 33: Enhancing Data Visualization with Interactivity and Animation

In the ever-evolving world of data visualization, static charts and graphs are no longer enough. Audiences crave dynamic and engaging experiences when digesting information. As technology advances, so do the ways in which we can present data, and one of the most effective methods is through interactive dashboards and animated data stories. These tools not only make data more visually appealing, but they also allow for a deeper understanding and engagement with the information. In this chapter, we will explore the power of interactivity and animation in data visualization and how it can enhance the user experience.

Interactive Dashboards

Interactive dashboards have become a staple in data visualization, allowing for a more immersive and personalized experience for users. These customized dashboards allow viewers to explore the data at their own pace and in the way that best suits their analytical needs. With a few clicks, users can drill down into specific data points, change parameters, and filter data to gain a deeper understanding of the information presented. This level of interactivity not only enhances understanding but also encourages users to engage with the data in a more meaningful way.Furthermore, interactive dashboards can also be adjusted and updated in real-time, giving users access to the most current data available. This can be particularly useful for businesses, as it allows for a more efficient decision-making process based on the most up-to-date information. Additionally, interactive dashboards can be shared and accessed online, making collaboration and information sharing easier than ever before.

Animated Data Stories

Animated data stories take data visualization to a whole new level. Rather than simply presenting static charts and graphs, these stories use animation to bring the data to life and tell a compelling narrative. By adding movement, color, and sound, the data becomes more engaging and captivating, capturing the audience's attention and keeping them invested in the information being presented.One of the advantages of animated data stories is the ability to convey complex data in a simple and digestible manner. By incorporating animation, the data can be broken down into smaller, more manageable pieces, making it easier for audiences to understand and retain the information. This makes it a valuable tool for presenting data to non-technical audiences who may struggle with traditional charts and graphs.

Engaging User Experience

Both interactive dashboards and animated data stories contribute to the overall user experience in data visualization. By combining interactivity and animation, users are able to fully immerse themselves in the data, leading to a more enjoyable and meaningful experience. Not only does this make the data more engaging, but it also promotes a deeper understanding and retention of the information presented. Moreover, by providing an engaging user experience, data visualization becomes more appealing and accessible to a wider audience. This can be especially useful for businesses or organizations looking to communicate their data to a broader demographic. By making the data more visually appealing and interactive, their message can reach a larger audience and have a more significant impact.

In conclusion, the use of interactivity and animation in data visualization enhances its effectiveness and captivates audiences in a way that traditional charts and graphs cannot. By creating customized and immersive experiences, interactive dashboards and animated data stories allow for a deeper understanding and engagement with the data. As technology continues to advance, we can only imagine the new and innovative ways in which data visualization will continue to evolve. But one thing is for sure - interactivity and animation have certainly become a vital part of creating actionable insights with data visualization and storytelling.

Chapter 34: Storytelling with Data using the Power of Emotion

In today's data-driven world, numbers and statistics often dominate our decision-making processes. However, studies have shown that emotional appeal can be just as persuasive, if not more, in influencing our actions. This is why utilizing emotional storytelling techniques in data visualization can be a powerful tool in driving action and change.

Emotional Appeal

Emotions are a universal language that connects us all. Just think about your favorite childhood story or the last movie that made you cry – these narratives tapped into your emotions and left a lasting impact. Similarly, when data is presented in a story format that evokes strong emotions, it becomes memorable and relatable.Data visualization allows us to bring data to life by creating a story around it. When done effectively, it can trigger an emotional response in the audience and make them feel connected to the data. This emotional appeal can encourage people to take action, whether it's donating to a cause, changing their behavior, or advocating for change.

Leveraging Empathy

Empathy is the ability to understand and share the feelings of another. It is a powerful force that drives us to take action for the greater good. By incorporating empathy into data visualization, we can create a deeper and more meaningful connection with the audience.For example, a visualization that shows the impact of climate change on a local community can be much more impactful than a chart with just numbers. By tapping into the feelings of empathy, the audience is more likely to relate to the data and feel compelled to make a change.

Tapping into Human Psychology

Human psychology plays a significant role in decision making. Emotions, biases, and cognitive processes all influence how we interpret and respond to information. By understanding these factors, we can craft data visualizations that are not only visually appealing but also emotionally persuasive. Visual cues such as color, images, and layout can evoke specific emotions and influence our perception of the data. Incorporating storytelling techniques like a narrative arc or a call to action can also tap into our psychological tendencies and influence our behavior. In addition, using data visualization to connect with our audience's core values and beliefs can also be a powerful tool. When we see data that aligns with our values, we are more likely to feel compelled to support or act on it.

In conclusion, emotions are a vital aspect of the human experience – they can motivate us to take action or inspire us to change. By incorporating emotional storytelling techniques into data visualization, we can create meaningful connections with our audience and drive them to make a difference. So next time you present data, remember to harness the power of emotion and tell a story that will leave a lasting impact.

Chapter 35: Visualizing Financial Data for Business Insights

Money, money, money. It's what makes the world go 'round, and it's also a crucial aspect of any business. As a business owner, understanding your financial data and making strategic decisions based on it is essential for success. However, numbers and spreadsheets can be overwhelming and difficult to comprehend for many people. This is where data visualization comes in – presenting financial data in a visually appealing and easy-to-understand way. In this chapter, we will explore how data visualization can be used for budgeting, financial forecasting, and identifying trends and patterns to gain valuable insights for your business.

Budgeting

Budgeting is a vital aspect of running a business. It involves carefully planning and managing your income and expenses, which can be a daunting task. But with data visualization, budgeting can become less intimidating and even enjoyable. By visually representing your financial data, you can clearly see where your money is going and where you can make adjustments to improve your bottom line.One way to use data visualization for budgeting is by creating a budget dashboard. This dashboard can display key financial metrics, such as revenue, expenses, and profits, in various charts and graphs. With a quick glance, you can see if any areas are overspending or underspending, allowing you to make necessary adjustments to keep your budget on track. You can also add filters to the dashboard to view data for specific time frames, departments, or products, providing a more comprehensive understanding of your business's financial health.

Financial Forecasting

Financial forecasting is the process of predicting your business's future financial performance based on historical data and market trends. It is crucial for making informed decisions and setting realistic goals for your business. However, traditional financial forecasting methods, such as spreadsheets, can be time-consuming and prone to errors. Data visualization can simplify and accelerate the forecasting process.By using data visualization tools, you can easily detect patterns and trends in your financial data, giving you a clearer picture of your business's financial future. With interactive visualizations, you can also input different scenarios, such as changes in market conditions or new products, to see how they would impact your financials. This allows you to make more accurate and strategic decisions for your business.

Identifying Trends and Patterns

Visualizing financial data can also help you identify trends and patterns that may not be apparent through numbers alone. Heat maps, line graphs, and bar charts can help you see which products are performing well, which ones need improvement, and which are losing money. This can help you allocate resources and make strategic decisions on where to invest and where to cut back.Data visualization can also help you identify spending patterns and analyze how each department is using your business's resources. With this information, you can identify areas of overspending and make necessary adjustments to reduce costs. You can also spot areas of potential growth and invest more resources to maximize profits.

Incorporating Data Visualization into Your Business Strategy

Incorporating data visualization into your business strategy can give you a competitive edge and keep you ahead of your competitors. With a clear and visual representation of your financial data, you can make informed decisions and identify opportunities that you may have otherwise missed. It can also help you communicate your financial goals and performance to stakeholders and investors, giving them a better understanding of your business's financial health.

Bringing It All Together

Budgeting, financial forecasting, and identifying trends and patterns are vital components of any successful business. Data visualization can transform these tasks from tedious and overwhelming to efficient and even enjoyable. With visually appealing and interactive representations of your financial data, you can gain valuable insights and make informed decisions to drive your business's success.So, embrace the power of data visualization and start using it to analyze your financial data. With the right tools and techniques, you can turn your financial data into a work of art that not only looks beautiful but also helps you take your business to new heights.

Chapter 36: Data Visualization for Non-Profit Organizations

Non-profit organizations play a crucial role in bringing about positive change in our society. They work tirelessly to address various social, environmental, and humanitarian issues. However, with limited resources and a constant need to attract donors and volunteers, these organizations face unique challenges in effectively communicating their impact and reach. This is where data visualization comes into play.

Adding an Element of Play

Data visualization can be a powerful tool for non-profits to engage with their audience and showcase their impact in a visually appealing and interactive manner. By adding an element of play to their data visualizations, these organizations can effectively capture the attention of potential donors and volunteers, making complex data more approachable and engaging.Imagine a virtual game where individuals can explore the various projects and initiatives undertaken by a non-profit organization. Through interactive visualizations, users can view real-time data on the number of people impacted by the organization, funds raised, and ongoing projects. This gamification of data can make the experience fun and engaging, encouraging users to explore and learn more about the organization's efforts.

Encouraging Exploration

Non-profit organizations often face the challenge of presenting large amounts of data to their audience without overwhelming them. Data visualization techniques can help break down complex information into digestible and visually appealing charts, graphs, and maps. These visual representations make it easier for individuals to explore and understand the data, encouraging them to delve deeper into the organization's initiatives and goals.For example, an interactive map can show the global reach of a non-profit organization's missions and projects. This not only provides a visual representation of their impact but also encourages users to explore further by clicking on different locations to view specific projects and their outcomes. This not only showcases the organization's reach but also highlights the diversity of their efforts.

Engaging Users

In today's digital world, individuals are bombarded with information from various sources. Non-profit organizations must find ways to stand out and engage with their audience effectively. Data visualization can help tell a powerful story, capturing the attention of potential donors and volunteers. By incorporating data storytelling techniques into their visualizations, non-profits can evoke an emotional response from their audience, making them more likely to take action and support the cause. An interactive data visualization that showcases the impact of an organization's efforts on individuals' lives can be a powerful tool to engage with potential donors and motivate them to contribute. Moreover, through data visualization, non-profit organizations can also provide transparency and accountability to their donors. A visually appealing and interactive dashboard can display real-time data on funds raised, expenses, and the impact of spending on projects. This level of transparency helps build trust and encourages individuals to support the organization's cause.

In conclusion, data visualization can be a game-changer for non-profit organizations. By adding an element of play, encouraging exploration, and engaging users, these organizations can effectively communicate their impact and reach, inspire individuals to support their cause, and drive positive change in our society. So, if you are a non-profit organization looking to make a bigger impact and attract more support, embrace the power of data visualization and tell your story like never before.

Chapter 37: Enhancing Donor Engagement and Measuring Impact with Data Visualization

Data visualization is more than just creating beautiful charts and graphs. It is the art of telling a story through data. And in the world of non-profit organizations, data storytelling is a crucial tool in engaging donors and measuring impact. In this chapter, we will explore how data visualization can be used to effectively communicate with donors, engage them in your cause, and measure the impact of your work.

Telling Stories with Data

As human beings, we are naturally drawn to stories. We connect with them on an emotional level and they have the power to inspire us, motivate us, and incite change. But when it comes to data, many non-profit organizations struggle to tell a compelling story. That's where data visualization comes in.With the use of charts, graphs, maps, and infographics, data visualization can turn raw numbers and statistics into a powerful narrative. It can take a complex data set and present it in a way that is visually appealing and easily understandable for donors. This not only helps in engaging donors, but also in building trust and credibility in the work of the organization.

Donor Engagement

One of the biggest challenges for non-profit organizations is engaging donors and keeping them invested in their cause. With the rise of social media and digital communication, donors are becoming more and more visual-oriented. They want to see the impact of their donations in a tangible and visual way. This is where data visualization can play a crucial role.By presenting data in a visually appealing way, donors can easily see the impact of their contributions. This not only creates a sense of satisfaction and trust in the organization, but also encourages them to continue supporting the cause. Data visualization can also be used as a marketing tool to attract new donors. By showcasing the success of the organization through data, it can inspire others to join in and support the cause.

Measuring Impact

Measuring the impact of a non-profit organization's work is essential in demonstrating the effectiveness of their programs and justifying their use of donor funds. However, with complex data and varying metrics, this can be a challenging task. Data visualization makes this process much more efficient and effective. Through interactive and dynamic visualizations, organizations can track and display their progress in real-time. This not only makes it easier for donors to understand the impact of their contributions, but also helps the organization to identify areas for improvement and strategize future initiatives.Additionally, data visualization can also help non-profits to communicate with stakeholders, such as government agencies and other organizations, in a more meaningful and impactful way. By presenting data visually, it becomes easier to convey the importance and urgency of the organization's cause and garner support.

Conclusion

Data storytelling is a powerful tool for non-profit organizations. It can help to engage donors, market the organization's work, and measure the impact of their programs. By using visually appealing data visualizations, organizations can effectively communicate with donors and stakeholders, build trust and credibility in their work, and ultimately make a greater impact in their cause. So don't just tell donors about your work, show them with the power of data visualization.

Chapter 38: Data Visualization For Non-Profit Organizations

Data-driven Storytelling: Communicating Impact Through Numbers and Visuals

In today's data-driven world, storytelling has become a crucial tool for non-profit organizations to communicate their impact and engage with their audiences. However, simply telling a story is no longer enough. With the abundance of data available, it is becoming increasingly important for non-profits to incorporate data-driven storytelling into their communication strategies.Data-driven storytelling involves using both data and narrative to tell a compelling story. It combines the power of numbers and visuals with the emotional connection of a story, resulting in a more impactful and persuasive message. By utilizing data, non-profit organizations can provide evidence and support for their cause, making their stories more credible and compelling.

Using Data to Support the Narrative Arc: Infusing Numbers into the Story

In order to effectively incorporate data into their storytelling, non-profits must first have a clear understanding of their narrative arc. The narrative arc is the foundation of any good story and involves the three basic elements: a beginning, middle, and end. For non-profits, the beginning is often the problem they are addressing, the middle is their efforts to solve the problem, and the end is the impact they have made.Once the narrative arc is established, using data to support each stage of the story is essential. For example, in the beginning, non-profits can use data to illustrate the severity of the problem and create a sense of urgency. In the middle, they can use data to showcase their efforts and progress. And in the end, they can use data to demonstrate the impact they have made and the positive change they have brought about.

Building a Cohesive Story: Visualizing Data for Maximum Impact

In addition to incorporating data into the narrative arc, non-profits must also present their data in a visually appealing and cohesive manner. This is where data visualization plays a crucial role. Visualizations can transform numbers and statistics into easily digestible and engaging visuals, making it easier for audiences to understand and connect with the data. Non-profit organizations can use a variety of data visualization techniques such as charts, graphs, maps, and infographics to present their data in a compelling way that supports their storytelling. These visualizations not only add depth and context to the story but also make it more memorable and shareable.Moreover, data visualizations can also help non-profits to uncover new insights and trends that may not have been apparent before. By exploring their data visually, organizations can gain a better understanding of their impact and make more informed decisions for the future.

Conclusion

Data-driven storytelling is a powerful tool for non-profit organizations to effectively communicate their impact and engage with their audiences. By infusing data into their narratives and presenting it through visualizations, non-profits can create a cohesive story that is both impactful and memorable. As the saying goes, "a picture is worth a thousand words", and in this case, data visualizations can convey the story of a non-profit's impact in a way that words alone cannot. So, for non-profits looking to make a difference and inspire change, incorporating data-driven storytelling is a must.

Chapter 39: Data Visualization for Human Resources and Recruitment

Identifying Talent

When it comes to human resources and recruitment, identifying the right talent is crucial for the success of any organization. However, traditional methods of evaluating candidates such as resumes and interviews can often be limiting and subjective. This is where data visualization can play a significant role in streamlining the hiring process and identifying top talent.With the help of data visualization, HR professionals can gain insights into candidates' skills, experience, and potential performance. By collecting and analyzing various data points, such as education, work history, and skills, visual representations can help in identifying patterns and identifying top performers. This not only saves time and effort in the hiring process but also ensures that the most suitable candidates are selected.

Analyzing Employee Data

In addition to hiring, data visualization also has a great impact on analyzing employee data. By visualizing data from employee surveys, performance reviews, and other HR metrics, HR professionals can gain a better understanding of their employees' needs and motivations.With interactive visualizations, HR professionals can drill down into specific data points to identify trends and patterns within the organization. This can help in identifying areas where employees may need more support or training, as well as recognizing top performers who may have previously gone unnoticed. By analyzing employee data through data visualization, HR professionals can make more informed decisions regarding employee development, retention, and overall organizational culture.

Improving Processes

Data visualization not only benefits HR professionals in identifying talent and analyzing employee data but also in improving overall processes within the organization. By visualizing data related to employee productivity, turnover rates, and other performance metrics, HR professionals can identify areas that need improvement and make data-driven decisions to enhance efficiency and productivity. For example, visualizing data on employee turnover rates can help identify the reasons for high turnover and take corrective measures to retain top talent. By analyzing data on employee efficiency, HR professionals can identify areas for improvement and make changes to optimize processes and increase productivity.Moreover, data visualization can also aid in evaluating the effectiveness of HR initiatives and training programs. By tracking and visualizing data related to these initiatives, HR professionals can assess their impact and make necessary adjustments for future programs.

The Power of Data Visualization in Human Resources

The use of data visualization in human resources is not just limited to hiring and performance evaluations. By incorporating data visualization into various HR processes and decisions, organizations can create a more efficient and engaged workforce. Moreover, data visualization can also contribute to creating a more transparent and inclusive workplace culture. By visualizing data related to diversity, inclusion, and employee satisfaction, HR professionals can identify areas for improvement and ensure equitable treatment for all employees.In today's fast-paced business world, data visualization has become an essential tool for HR professionals to make informed decisions and drive positive change within their organizations.

In Conclusion

Data visualization has emerged as a game-changer for human resources and recruitment. With its ability to simplify complex data, identify patterns, and provide actionable insights, it has revolutionized the way HR professionals approach their roles.From identifying top talent to streamlining processes and fostering an inclusive workplace culture, data visualization has the power to transform HR functions and contribute to the overall success of an organization. It is a tool that not only saves time and effort but also enhances decision-making and enables HR professionals to create a more engaged and productive workforce. So, embrace the power of data visualization in HR, and watch your organization thrive.

Chapter 40: Visualizing Data for Risk Management

As the digital age continues to evolve, the amount of data being generated and collected grows exponentially. This influx of data has given rise to the need for effective risk management strategies, as any business or organization must be prepared to mitigate potential threats and uncertainties. Data visualization has proven to be an invaluable tool in this process, allowing for a deeper understanding of risks and their potential impact. In this chapter, we will explore how data visualization can enhance risk management practices through immersive experiences and engaging with data in a new way.

Enhancing Data Storytelling

Data storytelling is the art of translating raw data into a captivating narrative that can drive decision-making. It is the key to unlocking the power of data visualization in risk management. Through methods such as infographics, charts, and interactive visuals, data storytelling takes complex data and presents it in a way that is easily digestible and memorable. This not only helps stakeholders grasp the severity of potential risks, but also allows them to visualize the data in a way that resonates on an emotional level, making it more likely to drive action.In risk management, data storytelling can reveal patterns and trends that may have otherwise gone unnoticed. By presenting data in a compelling way, it can garner attention and create a sense of urgency to address and mitigate risks. This results in more effective and timely risk management strategies that can help prevent or minimize potential damages.

Creating Immersive Experiences

Data visualization has become increasingly immersive, thanks to advances in technology and design. Virtual and augmented reality have opened up endless possibilities for risk management analysis, allowing for a more in-depth and interactive exploration of potential risks. These immersive experiences provide a new level of engagement with data, making it more meaningful and impactful.Interactive data visualizations in virtual reality can simulate different scenarios and allow stakeholders to see the potential effects of different risk management strategies. This hands-on approach not only helps them understand the data better, but also allows them to actively participate in the planning and decision-making process. This can lead to more effective risk management solutions that have been thoroughly tested and vetted through immersive experiences.

Engaging with Data in a New Way

In the past, risk management has primarily relied on analyzing historical data to identify potential threats and patterns. However, with the breadth of data available today, there are new opportunities to incorporate real-time data into risk management strategies. This allows for a more proactive approach to risk management, rather than a reactive one. Real-time data visualizations can provide up-to-date insights and allow for agile decision-making when it comes to risk management. By engaging with data in a new way, businesses and organizations can stay ahead of potential risks and take action before they become bigger issues. This also opens up the possibility for predictive analytics, where data visualizations can display potential future risks based on current data patterns.In addition, engaging with data in a new way can also include utilizing data from various sources, such as social media or customer feedback, to gain a more holistic view of potential risks. This can provide valuable insights that may have been overlooked with traditional risk management methods.

Risk Management in the Digital Age

Data visualization has revolutionized the way we approach risk management. It has made complex data more accessible and easier to understand, allowing for more effective risk management strategies. By enhancing data storytelling, creating immersive experiences, and engaging with data in a new way, businesses and organizations can stay ahead of potential risks and make more informed decisions. As we continue to advance technologically, the potential for data visualization in risk management only grows. It is crucial for any organization to embrace these capabilities and leverage them to their advantage in the ever-changing landscape of risk management in the digital age.

Chapter 41: Using Data Visualization for Risk Management

Identifying Potential Risks

When it comes to any business or organization, risk management is essential for mitigating potential issues and ensuring long-term success. However, identifying potential risks can be a daunting task, especially when dealing with large amounts of data. This is where data visualization can be a powerful tool in identifying potential risks and helping businesses make informed decisions. Through the use of charts, graphs, and other visual aids, data visualization allows for a comprehensive and organized view of potential risks. By visually presenting data, patterns and trends can be easily identified, allowing businesses to pinpoint areas that may require more attention and resources.In addition, data visualization allows for the exploration of different scenarios and potential outcomes. This can help businesses anticipate and prepare for potential risks in a proactive manner, rather than just reacting to them when they occur.

Communicating Risk Information

Once potential risks have been identified, it is important to effectively communicate this information to key stakeholders and decision-makers within the organization. This is where data visualization truly shines, as it allows for the effective and efficient communication of complex risk information. Visualizations can help to break down complex data into easily digestible and visually appealing forms, making it easier for non-technical individuals to understand and make informed decisions. This is especially important in risk management, as it allows for everyone within the organization to be on the same page and understand the potential risks at hand.Furthermore, data visualization can also help to communicate the severity and likelihood of potential risks. By using different colors or shapes to represent different levels of risk, data visualization can quickly convey the urgency of a particular situation and the potential impact on the organization.

Creating Strategies for Mitigation

One of the most significant benefits of using data visualization for risk management is the ability to create effective strategies for mitigation. As previously mentioned, data visualization can help businesses anticipate and prepare for potential risks, allowing for proactive decision-making. Through the use of interactive data visualizations, businesses can test different risk mitigation strategies and see how they may impact the overall outcome. This allows for a more data-driven approach to risk management, as decisions are based on real-time data and not just assumptions.In addition, data visualization also allows for the identification of trends and patterns in the data, which can help businesses make more informed decisions. By studying past data and visualizing potential future scenarios, businesses can make strategic decisions that can help mitigate risks and increase overall success. As we have explored in this chapter, data visualization can play a crucial role in risk management. From identifying potential risks to communicating them effectively and creating strategies for mitigation, data visualization is a valuable tool for businesses of all sizes and industries. However, as technology continues to evolve, it is important for businesses to stay updated and adapt to new tools and techniques in data visualization. This includes incorporating virtual and augmented reality into risk management processes, as well as utilizing machine learning and artificial intelligence for more accurate and predictive visualizations. Moreover, as the world becomes increasingly more data-driven, it is essential for businesses to prioritize data literacy and visualization skills. This means providing training and resources for employees to improve their understanding of data and how it can be used to make informed decisions.

In conclusion, data visualization has the potential to revolutionize the way businesses approach risk management. By leveraging the power of data and visual storytelling, businesses can make better-informed decisions, mitigate potential risks, and ultimately achieve long-term success.

Chapter 42: Tracking Progress, Identifying Obstacles, and Communicating Project Insights

In today's fast-paced world, project management has become an integral part of any successful business. With tight timelines and high expectations, it is crucial for project managers to constantly track progress, identify obstacles, and effectively communicate project insights to ensure the success of their projects. In this chapter, we will explore the importance of these three elements and how they can contribute to the overall success of a project.

Tracking Progress

Tracking progress is an essential aspect of project management. It involves continuously monitoring and evaluating the progress of a project to ensure that it is on track and meeting its objectives. This allows project managers to identify any potential issues or delays and take corrective actions before they become major problems. A project manager can track progress using various tools and techniques, such as project management software, timelines, project plans, and Gantt charts. These tools provide a visual representation of the project's progress, making it easier to identify any areas that need attention. By regularly monitoring progress, project managers can keep stakeholders informed and accountable, ensuring that tasks are completed on time to meet project deadlines.Tracking progress also allows project managers to make necessary adjustments to the project plan. By identifying any potential issues early on, project managers can modify the project plan to ensure that the project stays on track and within budget. This not only saves time and resources but also increases the chances of project success.

Identifying Obstacles

No project is without obstacles. When managing a project, it is essential to anticipate and identify potential obstacles that may arise. This allows project managers to plan and implement strategies to mitigate or overcome these obstacles before they significantly impact the project's progress. Identifying obstacles requires a proactive approach. Project managers must communicate and collaborate with their team to gain a thorough understanding of the project's goals and objectives. This will help them identify any potential risks that may arise and put measures in place to address them effectively.In addition to communication, project managers can also use risk management techniques to identify potential obstacles. Conducting risk assessments and creating risk management plans allows project managers to anticipate and prepare for any potential issues that may arise during the project's duration.

Communicating Project Insights

Effective communication is the cornerstone of successful project management. It involves sharing project insights and updates with stakeholders in a clear and concise manner. A project manager must be able to communicate project progress, challenges, and accomplishments with all stakeholders, including the project team, clients, and senior management. One of the most important aspects of communicating project insights is to provide regular updates. This not only keeps stakeholders informed but also allows project managers to gather feedback and make necessary adjustments to the project plan or strategy. Project managers should also tailor their communication to suit different audiences. For example, communicating project insights to team members may require more technical details, while communicating with clients may require a simplified and jargon-free approach. This will ensure that all stakeholders are on the same page and have a clear understanding of the project's progress. Another crucial aspect of communicating project insights is addressing and resolving any issues or concerns promptly. This not only builds trust and transparency among stakeholders but also demonstrates that the project manager is actively working towards the project's success.

In conclusion, tracking progress, identifying obstacles, and communicating project insights are all critical components of successful project management. They allow project managers to stay on track, anticipate potential issues, and keep stakeholders informed and engaged. By following these best practices, project managers can ensure the success of their projects and build a reputation as effective and efficient project leaders.

Chapter 43: Storytelling with Data for Personal Branding

Building Visual Resumes

In today's highly competitive job market, a traditional resume may not be enough to make you stand out from the rest of the candidates. Employers are looking for individuals who can not only list their skills and experiences but also showcase them in a visually appealing and engaging way. This is where a visual resume comes in. A visual resume is an innovative and powerful way to present your professional story. It uses images, graphics, and other visual elements to highlight your skills, achievements, and experiences. It can include infographics, data visualizations, and even videos to give employers a more comprehensive and memorable understanding of who you are as a professional.Creating a visual resume requires a combination of creativity and design skills. You can either hire a professional designer or use online tools and templates to create your own. Whichever route you choose, make sure your visual resume aligns with your personal brand and effectively communicates your skills and achievements.

Creating Personal Brand Stories

A personal brand story is a narrative that captures your unique identity, values, and experiences. It's an essential aspect of personal branding and can help you stand out in a crowded marketplace. Your personal brand story should highlight your strengths, passions, and achievements, and convey a clear message about who you are and what you stand for. When crafting your personal brand story, it's essential to consider your target audience and what they're looking for. Use your personal brand story to connect with your audience and build trust. Also, make sure it's authentic and genuine, as people are naturally drawn to stories that are personal and relatable.Your brand story should be consistent across all your professional platforms, including your website, social media profiles, and even your visual resume. This cohesive narrative will help create a strong and memorable personal brand that will attract the right opportunities to you.

Communicating Skills and Achievements

One of the most significant advantages of using data storytelling in personal branding is the ability to effectively communicate your skills and achievements. Instead of simply listing your qualifications and experiences on your resume, you can use data visualizations to showcase them in a more compelling and visually appealing way. For example, instead of stating that you're proficient in Microsoft Excel, you can create an infographic that shows your proficiency level, with charts and graphs to back it up. This approach not only makes your resume more engaging but also provides potential employers with concrete evidence of your skills.Additionally, storytelling through data visualization allows you to highlight your achievements and accomplishments in a visually impactful way. Instead of just stating the outcome, use visual elements to show the data and its impact. This will make a stronger case for your capabilities and make a lasting impression on potential employers.

Cultivating Your Personal Brand Through Storytelling with Data

Incorporating data storytelling into personal branding is a powerful way to cultivate a strong and memorable personal brand. It allows you to connect with your audience on a deeper level and effectively communicate your skills and achievements. With the increasing importance of digital presence and personal branding, using data storytelling can set you apart from the competition and help you achieve your professional goals.When using data storytelling for personal branding, it's important to maintain consistency and authenticity. Your personal brand story should align with your values and be reflected in all aspects of your professional life. Use your visual resume, personal brand story, and data visualizations to create a cohesive and compelling personal brand that will attract the right opportunities to you.

Achieving Success with Data Storytelling in Personal Branding

In conclusion, data storytelling is not just a powerful tool for businesses and organizations but also for individuals looking to build a strong personal brand. Craft your personal brand story, use data visualizations to communicate your skills and achievements, and maintain consistency and authenticity throughout your professional platforms. With the right combination of creativity, design, and storytelling, you can use data to showcase your capabilities and achieve success in your personal branding efforts.

Chapter 44: Visualizing Data for Environmental Impact

As we become more aware of the impact human activity has on our planet, it has become crucial to raise awareness and take action towards protecting the environment. However, understanding the complex data and trends related to environmental issues can be overwhelming. This is where the power of data visualization comes in – it allows us to see and understand the impact of our actions and make informed decisions for a better future.

Raising Awareness

Raising awareness is the first step towards any change, and visualizing data is an extremely effective way to do so. People are more likely to pay attention to and remember information when it is presented visually. By creating visually compelling graphics and infographics, we can capture people's attention and make them engage with environmental issues they may have never considered before.One of the greatest challenges in raising awareness for environmental issues is the disconnect between data and people's daily lives. Most of the time, data is presented in numbers and charts, making it difficult for people to relate to. But by incorporating visual elements such as images, videos, and interactive features, we can make the data more relatable and humanize the issue. This, in turn, can make people more likely to take action and make a difference.

Identifying Environmental Trends

Data visualization also plays a crucial role in identifying environmental trends and patterns. By analyzing and visualizing data, we can gain insights into the ever-changing state of our environment and identify key areas of concern. This information is crucial for policymakers, scientists, and individuals to understand the impact of climate change and the actions we need to take to mitigate it.Visualizing environmental trends can also help us make better predictions and inform decision-making. It allows us to track changes over time and make projections for the future. By presenting this data in a visually appealing manner, we can effectively communicate the urgency of taking action to protect our planet.

Communicating Solutions

In addition to raising awareness and identifying trends, data visualization also allows us to communicate solutions and inspire action. It is one thing to know the problem, but it is another to understand the solutions and how we can contribute to making a positive impact. By visualizing data on sustainable practices, renewable energy, and carbon footprints, we can educate people on concrete actions they can take in their daily lives to make a difference. This information can also be used to showcase successful case studies and motivate others to follow in their footsteps.Furthermore, data visualization can also be used in environmental campaigns and advocacy efforts. By presenting data in a visually appealing and easy-to-understand way, we can catch the attention of policymakers and decision-makers and urge them to take action towards creating a more sustainable future.

In Conclusion

Data visualization has the power to raise awareness, identify environmental trends, and communicate solutions for a better future. As we strive towards a more sustainable and eco-friendly world, visualizing data is crucial in understanding the impact of our actions and inspiring change. So let us harness the power of data visualization to protect our planet and create a brighter future for generations to come.

Chapter 45: The Power of Data Visualization in Environmental Impact

Data visualization is a powerful tool that not only helps us understand complex information, but also has the ability to drive significant change. In the context of environmental impact, data visualization plays a crucial role in conveying the urgency of sustainability and advocating for meaningful action. In this chapter, we will explore the importance of data visualization in addressing environmental issues, and how metrics and measurements, user feedback, and continuous improvement are key in creating impactful and actionable visualizations.

Metrics and Measurements

Metrics and measurements are essential elements in the field of environmental impact. They provide a quantitative understanding of the scale and severity of different environmental issues and help us track progress towards sustainability goals. However, raw data and numbers can be overwhelming and difficult for the general audience to comprehend. This is where data visualization comes in.Visualizing environmental data not only makes it easier for people to understand, but it also has the power to evoke emotions and drive action. For example, a simple line graph showing the rising levels of carbon emissions over the years can have a significant impact on people's perception of the climate crisis. By using visuals to present metrics and measurements, we can effectively communicate the urgency of environmental issues and create a sense of accountability for individuals, organizations, and governments.

User Feedback

One of the most powerful ways to improve the impact of data visualization in environmental issues is by incorporating user feedback. This involves collecting insights and input from the target audience or stakeholders and using it to improve the design and delivery of data-driven messages.Feedback from users can help identify gaps in understanding, suggest improvements in visuals, and provide valuable insights on how to make the data more relatable and relevant. For instance, if the target audience is not resonating with a particular visualization, gathering user feedback can help determine which elements need to be changed or improved. By using this feedback, we can create data visualizations that are not only visually appealing but also effective in conveying the message and driving action.

Continuous Improvement

Data visualization in environmental impact is not a one-time effort. As the landscape of sustainability and environmental issues continue to evolve, so should our visualizations. This is where the importance of continuous improvement comes in. By regularly monitoring and evaluating the impact of our visualizations, we can identify areas of improvement and make necessary changes to ensure they remain relevant and effective. Additionally, as technology advances, new and improved visualization techniques emerge, giving us the opportunity to constantly enhance and innovate our data-driven messaging.Incorporating continuous improvement also means constantly seeking out new data sources, improving data quality, and finding new and creative ways to present information. By doing so, we can keep up with the ever-changing environmental landscape and effectively communicate the most up-to-date data to our audience.

In Conclusion

In conclusion, data visualization is a powerful tool in addressing environmental impact. By using metrics and measurements, gathering user feedback, and continuously improving our visualizations, we can create impactful and actionable data-driven messages that drive change. As we continue to face pressing environmental issues, the power of data visualization will play a vital role in shaping our understanding and driving us towards a more sustainable future.

Chapter 46: Communicating Political Data through Visualization

When it comes to politics, effective communication is essential in shaping public opinion and influencing policy changes. With the increasing availability of data and the rise of visual storytelling, data visualization has become a powerful tool in communicating political information. In this chapter, we will explore how data visualization can be used to effectively communicate policies, visualize election data, and ultimately influence public opinion.

Communicating Policies

Politics is often a complex and dense topic, making it challenging for the general public to fully understand policies and their implications. This is where data visualization comes in. By using various visual elements such as charts, graphs, and maps, political data can be made more accessible and easier to comprehend. One of the main benefits of data visualization is its ability to present information in a visually compelling way. By using vibrant colors, interactive elements, and engaging design, data can be presented in a way that captures the attention of the audience and makes it more memorable. This is especially important in the political arena, where policymakers often rely on statistics to support their agendas. With data visualization, these statistics can be presented in a way that is more likely to resonate with the public and potentially sway their opinions.Moreover, data visualization also allows for the comparison of policies and their impact over time. By using visualizations such as line graphs or bar charts, it becomes easier to see the changes in policies, and the trends and patterns that emerge. This helps in evaluating the effectiveness of policies and provides a more comprehensive understanding of their implications.

Visualizing Election Data

Elections are a crucial aspect of politics, and data visualization can play a significant role in presenting election data in a meaningful way. By using visuals such as maps, charts, and infographics, election data can be visualized in a more engaging and understandable manner. One of the main uses of data visualization in elections is to track and present voting patterns. By mapping out the results of elections, data visualization can provide a clear picture of how different populations voted and how that impacted the overall outcome. This allows for a better understanding of the demographic and geographic influences on elections and provides valuable insights for future campaigns.In addition to tracking and mapping voting patterns, data visualization can also be used to present polling data. By using interactive charts and graphs, citizens can track poll results in real-time, providing them with valuable insights into the voting trends and potential outcomes. This can also serve as a tool for election education, as it allows for an in-depth exploration of the data and its implications.

Influencing Public Opinion

One of the most significant impacts of data visualization in politics is its ability to influence public opinion. By presenting data in a visually appealing and engaging way, it becomes much more accessible and easier to understand for the general public. This can have a significant impact on shaping public opinion and ultimately influencing policy changes. Visualizations, such as infographics, can be used to present compelling narratives that highlight the importance of specific policies or bring attention to societal issues. By weaving data and statistics into a story, visualizations can evoke emotions and ultimately influence the way people think about certain political topics.Furthermore, data visualization also allows for the exploration of different scenarios and their outcomes. By presenting policy data in an interactive format, citizens can explore the potential consequences of different policies, allowing them to make more informed decisions and potentially sway their opinions.

Conclusion

In today's fast-paced world, effective communication and the ability to capture people's attention are crucial in the political arena. Data visualization offers a powerful tool in communicating policies, visualizing election data, and influencing public opinion. By presenting data in an engaging and meaningful way, it becomes easier to understand and remember. This, in turn, can lead to more informed decision-making and potentially impact policy changes. As data visualization continues to evolve and advance, its role in politics will only continue to grow, making it an essential tool for effective communication and change.

Chapter 47: The Power of Data Visualization in Politics

Politics, a topic that can often incite heated debates and stir up intense emotions. It's no surprise that many people shy away from discussing it, let alone analyzing the vast amounts of data that go into it. But as the world becomes more connected and information becomes more accessible, data visualization is playing a crucial role in politics.

Personalization

One of the key elements that data visualization brings to politics is personalization. It allows voters to see the issues that affect them directly, in a way that is easily digestible and relatable. No longer do we have to sift through pages of numbers and statistics to understand the impact of policies or political decisions. Through data visualization, we can see how taxes, healthcare, and education, among other things, affect our daily lives.In today's political climate, personalization is more critical than ever. With the rise of social media and targeted advertising, politicians can now tailor their messages to specific demographics and sway their opinions with ease. But with data visualization, voters can see beyond the tailored messages and explore the facts for themselves, making more informed decisions.

Data-driven marketing

Data-driven marketing has been around for a while, but it's only in recent years that it's made its way into politics. By collecting and analyzing data on voter behavior and preferences, politicians can now create targeted campaigns that resonate with their audience. Data visualization plays a crucial role in this process, allowing politicians to present their data in a visually appealing and easy-to-understand way.Think of political ads and social media posts that you see during election season. Many of them use data visualization, whether it's through infographics, charts, or maps, to convey their message and make it more convincing. And as technology advances, we can expect to see even more sophisticated uses of data visualization in political marketing.

Tracking customer behavior

In the world of politics, voters are essentially customers. And like any business, politicians need to understand their customers' behavior to make informed decisions. This is where data visualization comes in handy. By tracking voter behavior and preferences, politicians can gain valuable insights into what issues matter most to their constituents.With data visualization, politicians can also track the effectiveness of their campaigns. By analyzing data on how voters respond to their messages, they can tailor their strategies to appeal to a broader audience. And with real-time data visualization, they can quickly adapt their campaigns as needed, maximizing their chances of success.

The future of data visualization in politics

As technology continues to advance, we can expect data visualization to play an even more significant role in politics. With the rise of artificial intelligence, politicians can now analyze vast amounts of data and gain insights that were once impossible to obtain. We can also expect to see more interactive and immersive data visualizations, making it easier for voters to engage with the political process. Moreover, the use of data visualization in politics can lead to more transparency and accountability. By presenting data in a clear and unbiased manner, politicians hold themselves more accountable for their decisions and actions. And voters can hold them accountable as well by making informed decisions based on the data presented.

In conclusion, we can see the immense potential of data visualization in politics. It has the power to personalize messages, drive data-driven marketing, and track customer behavior. As technology continues to advance, we can expect to see even more sophisticated uses of data visualization in the political arena. So the next time you see a chart or graph accompanying a political message, take a closer look, and you might just uncover some valuable insights.

Chapter 48: Leveraging Data Visualization for Competitive Intelligence

Data visualization has revolutionized the way we understand and analyze data, allowing us to identify patterns and insights that were previously hidden. In the world of business, this has become a valuable tool for gaining a competitive edge. By effectively visualizing data, companies can identify market trends, analyze competitor data, and forecast changes in the market. In this chapter, we will explore how data visualization can be leveraged for competitive intelligence, giving businesses the ability to make informed and strategic decisions.

Identifying Market Trends

In today's fast-paced world, markets are constantly evolving and shifting. It is crucial for businesses to stay on top of these changes in order to remain competitive. With data visualization, companies are able to not only analyze their own data, but also gather and visualize data from external sources. This allows them to identify trends and patterns in the market, giving them a deeper understanding of consumer behaviors and preferences.Gone are the days of tedious and time-consuming data analysis. With data visualization, powerful tools and software have been developed to retrieve and visualize data in a matter of minutes. This allows businesses to stay up-to-date with the latest market trends and make quicker decisions. By having a visual representation of the data, companies can spot patterns and trends that may have otherwise been missed, giving them a competitive advantage.

Analyzing Competitor Data

In addition to monitoring market trends, businesses can also use data visualization to analyze their competitors. By visualizing data from their competitors, companies can gain a comprehensive understanding of their strengths and weaknesses. This can help businesses benchmark their own performance and identify areas for improvement.Data visualization also allows businesses to compare their own data to that of their competitors, giving them a clear understanding of where they stand in the market.

Furthermore, by overlaying data from multiple competitors, companies can identify common trends and patterns, helping them make more informed decisions on their own strategies.

Forecasting Market Changes

The ability to predict market changes is an important factor in remaining competitive. Data visualization provides a real-time view of the market, making it easier for companies to recognize shifts and make predictive projections. By analyzing past and current market trends, businesses can make informed decisions on future strategies and objectives.Moreover, by incorporating machine learning and predictive analytics into data visualization, businesses can use historical data to forecast market changes and gain a competitive edge. They can also use these insights to identify opportunities for growth and innovation.

The Power of Data Visualization in Competitive Intelligence

Data visualization has changed the game for competitive intelligence. It allows businesses to analyze vast amounts of data with speed and accuracy, giving them a deeper understanding of their market and competitors. By leveraging data visualization, companies can make informed decisions and identify valuable insights that can be used to gain a competitive edge.Not only does data visualization make data easier to understand, but it also makes it more engaging and captivating. Through creative and dynamic visualizations, businesses can communicate complex data in a way that is both informative and aesthetically pleasing. This can help businesses stand out from their competitors and make a lasting impression on their audience.

The Future of Data Visualization in Competitive Intelligence

As technology continues to advance, we can expect to see even more innovations in data visualization for competitive intelligence. Virtual and augmented reality, for example, have the potential to transform how we interact with data. With these advanced technologies, businesses can create immersive and interactive data visualizations, allowing for a deeper understanding and analysis of complex data sets.Data visualization will also continue to play a vital role in the integration of machine learning and AI in competitive intelligence. These technologies have the ability to process and analyze large amounts of data at lightning speed, giving businesses valuable insights and predictions in real-time.

In Conclusion

Data visualization has become a critical tool in competitive intelligence, giving businesses the ability to identify market trends, analyze competitor data, and forecast changes in the market. By using powerful visualization tools and incorporating new technologies, businesses can make informed decisions and gain a competitive edge. As we continue to advance in the world of data and technology, it is clear that data visualization will play an even greater role in shaping the future of competitive intelligence.

Chapter 49: Communicating Complex Data through Visualization

Communicating Complex Data

As technology continues to advance and the amount of data grows exponentially, it is becoming increasingly difficult to effectively communicate complex data to the general public. While many individuals have some level of understanding when it comes to basic statistics and data analysis, it can be overwhelming for them to make sense of large datasets and complex research findings. This is where data visualization comes in – a powerful tool to simplify and convey important information in a way that is easy to understand and visually appealing.Data visualization is more than simply creating charts and graphs, it is a combination of art and science. It involves choosing the right visualizations to represent the data in the most accurate and effective way, while also telling a cohesive story. As a data storyteller, it is your job to bridge the gap between the raw data and the audience, making sure that the message is clear and engaging.

Visualizing Research Findings

Research findings are the cornerstone of any scientific or academic work. However, it is not enough to simply publish these findings in academic journals – they must also be communicated to a wider audience. This is where data visualization can be incredibly helpful. By taking the complex research and turning it into easily understandable visuals, it becomes more accessible and relatable to the general public.The key to effective visualization of research findings is understanding your audience. Different demographics may require different visualizations and storytelling techniques. For example, you might use more interactive and engaging visualizations for a younger audience, while a more traditional approach may be more appropriate for an older demographic. Knowing how to communicate your research findings through visualization is essential for garnering the attention and understanding of your audience.

Engaging with the Public

In today's fast-paced and information-filled world, it can be a challenge to capture and maintain the attention of the general public. This is why data visualization is such a valuable tool for engaging with the public. It allows you to present complex information in a visually appealing and captivating way, making it more likely to resonate with your audience. Visuals have the power to evoke emotions and spark a connection with the audience, and when used in combination with storytelling, can create a powerful impact. This can lead to increased interest and engagement with your data, as well as a better understanding and appreciation of the message you are trying to convey. Engaging with the public through data visualization not only benefits your research, but it also helps to promote data literacy and raise awareness of important issues.

In conclusion, data visualization is a crucial tool for effectively communicating complex data. It combines art and science to bridge the gap between data and the general public, making it more accessible and engaging. By understanding your audience, visualizing research findings, and engaging with the public, you can create impactful visual stories that not only communicate important data but also capture the attention and interest of your audience. Keep exploring and innovating with data visualization to pave the way for a more visually literate and informed society.

www.ingramcontent.com/pod-product-compliance
Lightning Source LLC
LaVergne TN
LVHW051705050326
832903LV00032B/4017